ESSENTIAL BIBLIOGRAPHY OF AMERICAN FICTION

MODERN AFRICAN AMERICAN WRITERS

ESSENTIAL BIBLIOGRAPHY OF AMERICAN FICTION

MODERN AFRICAN AMERICAN WRITERS

Matthew J. Bruccoli and
Judith S. Baughman,
Series Editors

Foreword by Keneth Kinnamon

Facts On File®

AN INFOBASE HOLDINGS COMPANY

MODERN AFRICAN AMERICAN WRITERS
Copyright © 1994 by Manly, Inc. and Facts On File, Inc.

Facts On File, Inc.
460 Park Avenue South
New York NY 10016

Library of Congress Cataloging-in-Publication Data

Modern African American writers / Matthew J. Bruccoli and Judith S. Baughman, series editors; foreword by Keneth Kinnamon.
p. cm. — (Essential bibliography of American fiction)
Includes index.
ISBN 0-8160-2998-9 (HC). — ISBN 0-8160-2999-7 (PB)
1. American fiction—Afro-American authors—History and criticism—Bibliography. 2. American fiction—Afro-american authors—Bibliography. 3. Afro-Americans in literature—Bibliography. I. Bruccoli, Matthew Joseph, 1931- . II. Baughman, Judith. III. Series.
Z1229.N39M63 1993
[PS374.N4]
016.813'509896—dc20   93-8643

A British CIP catalogue record for this book is available from the British Library.

Facts On File books are available at special discounts when purchased in bulk quantities for businesses, associations, institutions or sales promotions. Please call our Special Sales Department in New York at 212/683-2244 or 800/322-8755.

Text design by Catherine Hyman
Cover design by Heidi Haeuser
Composition by Grace M. Ferrara/Facts On File, Inc.
Manufactured by the Maple-Vail Book Manufacturing Group

Printed in the United States of America

10 9 8 7 6 5 4 3 2 1

This book is printed on acid-free paper.

CONTENTS

SERIES INTRODUCTION

These volumes in the *Essential Bibliography of American Fiction* series are largely adapted from author entries in *Facts On File Bibliography of American Fiction, 1919–1988* (1991) and *Facts On File Bibliography of American Fiction, 1866–1918* (1993), known as *BAF*. The *Essential Bibliography of American Fiction* makes *BAF* material on certain widely read and widely studied authors available in a more affordable format. Whereas *BAF* is intended for colleges and university research libraries, the *Essential Bibliography of American Fiction* volumes are revised for high schools, community colleges, and general libraries—as well as for classroom use.

None of the author entries in this new series is a direct reprint from *BAF*. Each entry has been updated to the end of 1992. The primary bibliographies are complete, but the secondary bibliographies have been trimmed. The *Essential Bibliography of American Fiction* entries are modified for general usability by a cross-section of students, teachers, and serious readers. Asterisks now identify the most generally available and most influential secondary books and articles. The asterisks do not designate the best works—which is a matter for argument; the asterisks mark what can be described as "standard" biographical and critical works.

To enhance the usefulness of the *Essential Bibliography of American Fiction* new entries have been compiled for authors who are not in *BAF*—notably, writers born after 1940.

The authors in each *Essential Bibliography of American Fiction* volume are eminent fiction writers who have been grouped on the basis of their backgrounds and materials. The selection of the figures was made in consultation with teachers and librarians. Since a writer will appear in only one volume, it was necessary to decide in which of several possible volumes a figure should be placed: Toni Morrison, for example, was assigned to *African American Writers* rather than to *Women Writers*.

Mark Twain declared that ". . . almost the most prodigious asset of a country, and perhaps its most precious possession, is its native literary product—when that product is free and noble and enduring." The power of literature requires collaboration between authors and their readers. The *Essential Bibliography of American Fiction* series endeavors to promote that collaboration.

FOREWORD

Until the beginning of the twentieth century, American literature was, for the most part, the exclusive province of white writers of Protestant origin, mostly male, mainly of the eastern seaboard, and principally of British descent. They had such names as Mather, Edwards, Franklin, Irving, Cooper, Emerson, Poe, Simms, Hawthorne, Melville, Stowe, Whitman, Dickinson, Adams, and James. Such Huguenot names as Freneau and Thoreau were exceptions to this generalization. As for geographical origin, more than half of those listed were born in Boston or New York; the others first saw the light seventy miles or closer to the Atlantic Ocean. Voices from the Middle West were not heard before Samuel Langhorne Clemens and William Dean Howells emerged from Missouri and Ohio just before the Civil War, and both of these authors spent most of their adult lives in the Northeast.

To a large degree these patterns were determined by the demographic facts. British colonial settlement hugged the coast for two centuries before venturing westward. Boston, New York, Philadelphia, Charleston—these were the centers of literacy, education, and the publishing trade, all necessary for the development of printed literature. After the Revolution, political power was held almost exclusively by white males of Protestant background. WASP—White Anglo-Saxon Protestant—is more than a label; it is an accurate identification of those who controlled the government of the United States and wrote its books until the twentieth century. But ethnocentrism (belief that one's own group is superior) was more than a reflection of the historical process. It was also a doctrine consciously held, the nationalist and racist narrowness of which unduly restricted for too long a time our understanding of what constitutes the literature of the North American continent or even of the landmass north of Mexico and south of Canada. This is not to say that the fiction of Melville, James, and Hemingway or the poetry of Whitman, Dickinson, and Frost should be in any way neglected. It *is* to say that the oral and written literature of Native Americans, the Spanish-speaking peoples of the Southwest, the Creoles and Cajuns of the Louisiana territory, as well as the more recent literature of twentieth-century immigrants from eastern and southern Europe should all be considered as part of our multicultural national heritage. Above all, attention is due to the most copious, the oldest, the most historically significant, the most socially relevant, and the most aesthetically satisfying, after the English American, of all our national literatures—that of African Americans.

Some might argue that the oral literary tradition of African Americans began with Estevanico, an African Spanish soldier in the troops of the conquistador Coronado's 1540 expedition into what is now Arizona, New

Mexico, Texas, Oklahoma, and Kansas. African French were among the explorers and settlers of the Mississippi River Valley in the seventeenth and eighteenth centuries. One of them, Jean Baptiste Point du Sable, established in 1779 a trading post on Lake Michigan that eventually grew into the city of Chicago. Africans first arrived in an English colony when a Dutch ship brought twenty slaves to Jamestown in 1619, the year before the Pilgrims reached Plymouth. Most Africans transported to the New World came in chains, lived in bondage to whites, and had little or no access to a condition of literacy. Their literature was perforce oral and originally African, but as the generations progressed, African folklore was adapted to the American environment, resulting in a rich oral tradition that has continued now for close to four hundred years. Rap is only one of its contemporary forms.

Formal written literature in English by African Americans began in the latter half of the eighteenth century, when the major figures were the stylistically accomplished Phillis Wheatley and the fascinating autobiographer Olaudah Equiano, both African born. In the nineteenth century there was abundant black literary activity, most of its addressing the issues of slavery and racism. Frederick Douglass, racial leader, superb autobiographer, abolitionist newspaperman, and brilliant orator, is the central African American figure of the century. Born in slavery, he ascended to literacy, indeed to literary mastery, with *Narrative of the Life of Frederick Douglass, an American Slave* (1845), beginning a public career that was to continue for fifty years. Among the dozens of other African American writers of the time, even a brief account must mention Alexander Crummell, the Episcopalian clergyman, who divided his life among America, England, and Liberia; William Wells Brown, a versatile man of letters; Frances E. Watkins Harper, poet and novelist; the historian George Washington Williams; the renowned racial leader and autobiographer Booker T. Washington; and, especially, the popular poet and fiction writer Paul Laurence Dunbar.

The twentieth century has witnessed a virtual explosion of black literary productivity. Continuing careers begun in the waning years of the nineteenth century, Dunbar and Washington lived on until 1906 and 1915 respectively. Their accomplished contemporary Charles W. Chesnutt published his first short story in 1887 and his short biography of Douglass and his two collections of short stories in 1899, but his three novels appeared early in the new century. A master of irony, Chesnutt is the best African American novelist until the advent of Zora Neale Hurston and Richard Wright in the 1930s. The other great name in the years before World War I was W. E. B. Du Bois, whose long life (1868–1963), brilliant mind, and indefatigable energy made him the most imposing black intellectual in American history. Historian, sociologist, biographer, autobiographer, poet, novelist, journalist, Du Bois was the most versatile and one of the most perceptive of all the analysts of what he called in his best book *The Souls of Black Folk* (1903). Similar in his versatility and a better poet and novelist was James Weldon Johnson, who became one of the elder figures in that creative ferment of the 1920s that came to be known as the Harlem Renaissance. Other major participants in this movement were Claude McKay, Jamaica-born poet and novelist, who traveled from Bolshevism to the Roman Catholic faith; Jean Toomer, near-white mystic whose *Cane* (1923) is one of the strangest and most beautiful books in the African American canon; Langston Hughes, an excellent poet who also wrote in other genres; and Countee Cullen, a polished poet deeply attracted to Romantic themes.

Zora Neale Hurston was born in 1901, making her just slightly older than the precocious Hughes and Cullen, but her literary talent required longer to incubate, her first book not appearing until 1934. A trained anthropologist, she has not been excelled in her presentation of black folklore. Of her three novels, *Their Eyes Were Watching God* (1937) remains the classic expression of black literary feminism. Richard Wright, though, was the dominant African American writer from 1938, when his first book appeared, until his death in Paris in 1960. A writer of overwhelming power and fierce protest, he was the most famous and the most widely read black writer in the world. Wright's *Native Son* (1940) and *Black Boy* (1945) are safe bets to be read as long as American books are read. Wright's younger friends and admirers, Ralph Ellison and James Baldwin, themselves went on to achieve literary fame, Ellison with the major novel *Invisible Man* (1952) and Baldwin with brilliant and beautifully written essays as well as six novels and other writings.

African American Literature has been characterized in the last three decades first by miltant protest and then by work of increasing complexity and maturity. Melvin B. Tolson, Robert Hayden, Gwendolyn Brooks, Amiri Baraka, Michael Harper, and Rita Dove in poetry; Lorraine Hansberry, Baraka, and Ed Bullins in drama; and Paule Marshall, Ernest Gaines, Alice Walker, Gloria Naylor, Ishmael Reed, John Wideman, and, especially, Toni Morrison in fiction are among the outstanding writers of this period. Concurrently with the development of these writers came increasing skill and sophistication on the part of critics interpreting their work and that of their predecessors. In addition to critical studies, excellent biographies now exist for many of the twentieth-century writers mentioned here.

To understand America one must have some understanding of the many cultures that make it up. Of these, African American culture is one of the largest, longest, and most important. The most rewarding approach to the culture, perhaps, is through its literature. Beyond the opportunity it provides for cultural understanding, however, good literature offers to the individual reader the intense pleasure aroused by memorable imaginative expression of human feelings, aspirations, situations, and conflicts that appear in all cultures. The purpose of this book is to facilitate access to writings by and about African American writers who both represent their culture and excel as literary artists.

>—*Keneth Kinnamon*
>Ethel Pumphrey Stephens Professor of English
>University of Arkansas

USING THE *ESSENTIAL BIBLIOGRAPHY OF AMERICAN FICTION*

The only basis for the full understanding and proper judgment of any author is what the writer wrote. In order to grasp the significance and value of a literary career, it is necessary to have a sense of the author's body of work. Bibliographies—lists of what the author wrote and what has been published about the author and the author's work—are the crucial tools of literary study.

The reader should always begin with the *primary* bibliography (the list of books *by* the author). What the author wrote is always much more important than what has been written about the works. Everything comes from the works themselves. Great fiction is much more than plot or story. The capacity of literature to move, excite, or gratify the reader results from the writing itself. Every great writer writes like no one else.

Yet writings about a work of literature may enlarge the reader's understanding. There is a point in the study of literature when the reader—in or out of the classroom—needs the help provided by sound, usable scholarship. Criticism varies greatly in its sense and utility. The best critics act as trustworthy intermediaries between the work and the reader, but the reader has the right to reject unhelpful critical material.

After reading the story or novel, the researcher should first consult a comprehensive bibliography of writings about the author's life and work—as cited in the *Essential Bibliography of American Fiction* (EBAF). An annotated secondary bibliography will provide brief indications of the content of articles and books. Thus a student seeking sources for a critical analysis of Zora Neale Hurston's *Their Eyes Were Watching God* should consult Adele S. Newson's *Zora Neale Hurston: A Reference Guide,* which describes seventy-two books, book sections, and articles between 1937 and 1986 that mention or focus on this novel. By checking promising *EBAF* Hurston items against Newson's annotations for these items, the researcher should be able to identify the most interesting or useful of these secondary materials. The most accessible and influential book-length studies are marked in *EBAF* by asterisks; almost all of these books have indexes, which will help students easily locate discussions of Hurston's novel.

Literary biography is not a substitute for the works; but biography augments the understanding of individual works and their function in the author's total achievement. Dr. Samuel Johnson, the great eighteenth-century literary biographer, observed that just as a soldier's life proceeds from battle to battle, so does a writer's life proceed from book to book. The more the reader knows about the writer, the more fully the reader will recognize the material for the fictions.

The author entries in *EBAF* provide guides for extended study of each writer's life and work; that is, they function as tutors for lifetime reading. Knowledge propagates knowledge. All literary activity is a process of discovery. In literary study it is crucial that students connect what they are reading with what they have previously read. Willing readers and students have been impeded by the inability to find out what to read next—or where to look for the answers to their questions. Reference books are portable universities. The *Essential Bibliography of American Fiction* provides keys to reference tools for the writers who secured the genius of American fiction.

PLAN OF THE ENTRIES

All authors selected for the *Essential Bibliography of American Fiction* receive the same treatment. No attempt has been made to indicate the stature of an author by the form of the entry. The length and scope of each entry is determined by the author's career.

The brief headnotes on the entries place the authors in terms of their reputations in their own time and now.

The first section of each author entry is reserved for BIBLIOGRAPHIES. Author bibliographies are traditionally divided into *primary works* (by the author) and *secondary works* (about the author).

The PRIMARY MATERIAL list in each entry begins with all BOOKS written by the subject author, as well as books for which the author had a major responsibility (as a collaborator or a ghost-writer). The next primary section includes LETTERS, DIARIES, NOTEBOOKS and is usually restricted to book-length works. The third primary section, OTHER, includes volumes in which the subject author was involved as contributor, editor, or translator; this list is selective. The final primary section, EDITIONS & COLLECTIONS, includes standard one-volume gatherings and multi-volume editions.

The MANUSCRIPTS & ARCHIVES section identifies the principal holdings of the author's manuscripts, typescripts, letters, and private papers in libraries or other institutional repositories.

A CONCORDANCE is an index of the words in a work or works by an author. Concordances are irreplaceable tools for the study of style and imagery.

The BIOGRAPHIES section is divided into three parts: *Books, Book Sections,* and *Articles* that focus on the author's career rather than on assessments of his or her work. This section is usually followed by INTERVIEWS, which includes book-length collections of interviews and single interviews of special interest.

The section of CRITICAL STUDIES is divided into five parts:

1. *Critical Books;*
2. Book-length *Collections of Essays* by various critics on the author or a single work by the author;
3. *Special Journals* devoted to an author (*Hemingway Review, Flannery O'Connor Bulletin*), as well as single issues of general scholarly journals (*Modern Fiction Studies*) dealing with that author;
4. *Book Sections* of volumes that treat several authors;
5. Journal or newspaper *Articles* that are critical rather than biographical.

In selecting articles, the contributors and editors have kept the resources and requirements of smaller libraries in mind. However, the most influential articles are always included.

TABLE OF ABBREVIATIONS

& c = and other cities
ed = editor or edited by
et al = and others
nd = no date provided
no = number
nos = numbers
Npl = no place of publication provided in the work
npub = no publisher provided in the work
ns = new series
P = Press
passim = throughout the volume
pp = pages
Repub = republished
Rev = revised
Rpt = reprinted
Sect = Section
U = University
U P = University Press
Vol = Volume

The following acronyms are the actual titles of journals

CLIO
ELH
MELUS
PMLA

JAMES BALDWIN

New York City, NY, 2 Aug 1924–St Paul de Vence, France, 1 Dec 1987

James Baldwin lived abroad for many years, primarily in France, but he never wavered from the conviction expressed early in his career: "I am an American writer. This country is my subject." As an essayist, novelist, dramatist, poet, and civil rights activist, Baldwin elicited strong responses because of his controversial convictions and his candor; an artist is "an incorrigible disturber of the peace," he said, thus confronting the dilemma "to be immoral and uphold the status quo or to be moral and try to change the world." By the time of his death Baldwin had achieved an international reputation as a man of letters.

Bibliographies

Bobia, Rosa M Williamson. "Annotated Bibliography of Francophone Sources on JB 1952–1981." *JB and His Francophone Critics: An Analysis and Annotated Bibliography (1952–1981)* (Ann Arbor, Mich: UMI, 1986), 113–198. Secondary.

*Smith, James F. "JB." *Contemporary Authors Bibliographical Series: American Novelists,* ed James J Martine (Detroit: Bruccoli Clark/Gale, 1986), 3–41. Primary & secondary; includes essay on secondary sources.

Standley, Fred L & Nancy V. *JB: A Reference Guide.* Boston: Hall, 1980. Secondary.

Books

Go Tell It on the Mountain. NY: Knopf, 1953. Novel.

Notes of a Native Son. Boston: Beacon, 1955. Rpt with intro by JB, 1984. Essays.

Giovanni's Room. NY: Dial, 1956. Novel.

Nobody Knows My Name: More Notes of a Native Son. NY: Dial, 1961. Essays.

Another Country. NY: Dial, 1962. Novel.

The Fire Next Time. NY: Dial, 1963. Essays.

Blues for Mister Charlie. NY: Dial, 1964. Play.

Nothing Personal, photos by Richard Avedon. NY: Atheneum, 1964.

Going to Meet the Man. NY: Dial, 1965. Stories.

The Amen Corner. NY: Dial, 1968. Play.

Tell Me How Long the Train's Been Gone. NY: Dial, 1968. Novel.

A Rap on Race: Margaret Mead and JB. Philadelphia & NY: Lippincott, 1971. Dialogue.

No Name in the Street. NY: Dial, 1972. Essays.

One Day, When I Was Lost: A Scenario Based on "The Autobiography of Malcolm X." London: Joseph, 1972; NY: Dial, 1973. Screenplay.

A Dialogue: JB and Nikki Giovanni. Philadelphia & NY: Lippincott, 1973.

If Beale Street Could Talk. NY: Dial, 1974. Novel.

Little Man, Little Man: A Story of Childhood. NY: Dial, 1976.

The Devil Finds Work: An Essay. NY: Dial, 1976.

Just Above My Head. NY: Dial, 1979. Novel.

Jimmy's Blues: Selected Poems. London: Joseph, 1983; NY: St Martin, 1986.

The Evidence of Things Not Seen. NY: Holt, Rinehart & Winston, 1985. Essay.

The Price of the Ticket: Collected Nonfiction 1948–1985. NY: St Martin/Marek, 1985.

Biographies

BOOKS

Campbell, James. *Talking at the Gates: A Life of JB.* NY: Viking, 1991.

Eckman, Fern Marja. *The Furious Passage of JB.* NY: Evans, 1966.

Edwards, David & Ian H Birnie. *JB and North America.* London: SCM, 1975.

Weatherby, W J. *JB: Artist on Fire.* NY: Fine, 1989.

ARTICLES

Howard, Jane. "Doom and Glory of Knowing Who You Are." *Life,* 54 (24 May 1963), 86B, 88–90.

Morrison, Allan. "The Angriest Young Man." *Ebony,* 16 (Oct 1961), 23–26, 28, 30.

Steinem, Gloria. "JB, an Original: A Sharpened View of Him." *Vogue,* 144 (Jul 1964), 78–79, 129, 138.

Interviews

BOOK

*Standley, Fred L & Louis H Pratt, eds. *Conversations With JB.* Jackson: U P Mississippi, 1989.

ARTICLES

"Liberalism and the Negro: A Round-Table Discussion," with JB, Nathan Glazer, Sidney Hook & Gunnar Myrdal. *Commentary,* 37 (Mar 1964), 25–42

"Dialogue in Black and White: JB and Budd Schulberg." *Playboy,* 13 (Dec 1966), 133–136, 282, 284, 286–287. Rpt Troupe.

"To Hear Another Language: A Conversation With Alvin Ailey, JB, Romare Beardon, and Albert Murray." *Callaloo,* 12 (Summer 1989), 431–452.

Critical Studies

BOOKS

*Harris, Trudier. *Black Women in the Fiction of JB.* Knoxville: U Tennessee P, 1985.

Macebuh, Stanley. *JB: A Critical Study.* NY: Third/ Okpaku, 1973.

Moller, Karin. *The Theme of Identity in the Essays of JB: An Interpretation.* Göteborg, Sweden: Acta Universitatis Gothoburgensis, 1975.

*Porter, Horace A. *Stealing the Fire: The Art and Protest of JB*. Middletown, Conn: Wesleyan U P, 1989.

Pratt, Louis H. *JB*. Boston: Twayne, 1978.

*Sylvander, Carolyn Wedin. *JB*. NY: Ungar, 1980.

Weatherby, W J. *Squaring Off: Mailer vs. B*. NY: Mason/Charter, 1977.

COLLECTIONS OF ESSAYS

Bloom, Harold, ed. *JB*. NY: Chelsea House, 1986.

Gibson, Donald, ed. *Five Black Writers: Essays on Wright, Ellison, B, Hughes, and LeRoi Jones*. NY: NYU P, 1970.

Kinnamon, Keneth, ed. *JB: A Collection of Critical Essays*. Englewood Cliffs, NJ: Prentice-Hall, 1974.

O'Daniel, Therman B, ed. *JB: A Critical Evaluation*. Washington: Howard U P, 1977.

*Standley, Fred L & Nancy V Burt, eds. *Critical Essays on JB*. Boston: Hall, 1988.

*Troupe, Quincy, ed. *JB: The Legacy*. NY: Simon & Schuster, 1989.

BOOK SECTIONS

Adams, Stephen. "JB." *The Homosexual as Hero in Contemporary Fiction* (Totowa, NJ: Barnes & Noble, 1980), 35–55. Rpt as "Giovanni's Room: The Homosexual as Hero," Bloom.

Allen, Shirley S. "The Ironic Voice in B's *Go Tell It on the Mountain*." O'Daniel, 30-37.

*Bell, Bernard W. "JAB." *The Afro-American Novel and Its Tradition* (Amherst: U Massachusetts P, 1987), 215–234.

Berghahn, Marion. "The Transitional Phase—Time of Skepticism." *Images of Africa in Black American Literature* (London: Macmillan, 1977), 152–188. Rpt as "Images of Africa in the Writings of JB," Bloom.

Brooks, A Russell. "JB as Poet-Prophet." O'Daniel, 126-134.

Cunningham, James. "Public and Private Rhetorical Modes in the Essays of JB." *Essays on the Essay: Redefining the Genre,* ed Alexander J Butrym (Athens: U Georgia P, 1989), 192–204.

Farrison, William Edward. "If B's Train Has Not Gone." O'Daniel, 69–81.

Ford, Nick Aaron. "The Evolution of JB as Essayist." O'Daniel, 85–104.

*Gibson, Donald B. "Ralph Ellison and JB." *The Politics of Twentieth-Century Novelists,* ed George A Panichas (NY: Hawthorn, 1971), 307–320.

Gibson. "JB: The Political Anatomy of Space." O'Daniel, 3–18.

Hakutani, Yoshinobu. "*No Name in the Street:* JB's Image of the American Sixties." Standley & Burt, 277–289.

Harper, Howard, Jr. "JB—Art or Propaganda?" *Desperate Faith: A Study of Bellow, Salinger, Mailer, B, and Updike* (Chapel Hill: U North Carolina P, 1967), 137–161.

Hernton, Calvin C. "Blood of the Lamb: The Ordeal of JB." *Amistad I,* ed John A Williams & Charles F Harris (NY: Vintage, 1970), 183–199.

Hernton. "A Fiery Baptism: Postscript." *Amistad I,* ed John A Williams & Charles F Harris (NY: Vintage, 1970), 200–225. Rpt Kinnamon.

Hernton. "JB: Dialogue and Vision." *American Writing Today,* ed Richard Kostelanetz (Troy, NY: Whitston, rev 1991), 245–253.

*Jarrett, Hobart. "From a Region in My Mind: The Essays of JB." O'Daniel, 105–125.

Jones, Harry L. "Style, Form and Content in the Short Fiction of JB." O'Daniel, 143–150.

Klein, Marcus. "JB: A Question of Identity." *After Alienation* (Cleveland: World, 1962), 147–195. Rpt Bloom.

Lee, Brian. "JB: Caliban to Prospero." *The Black American Writer,* Vol 1, ed C W E Bigsby (De Land, Fla: Everett/Edwards, 1969), 169–179.

Meserve, Walter. "JB's 'Agony Way.'" *The Black American Writer,* Vol 2, ed C W E Bigsby (De Land, Fla: Everett/Edwards, 1969), 171–186.

Millican, Arthenia Bates. "Fire as the Symbol of a Leading Existence in 'Going to Meet the Man.'" O'Daniel, 170–180.

*Molette, Carlton W. "JB as Playwright." O'Daniel, 183–188.

Murray, Albert. "JB, Protest Fiction, and the Blues Tradition." *The Omni-Americans* (NY: Outerbridge & Dienstfrey, 1970), 142–168.

*O'Neale, Sandra A. "Fathers, Gods, and Religion: Perceptions of Christianity and Ethnic Faith in JB." Standley & Burt, 125–143.

Orsagh, Jacqueline E. "B's Female Characters: A Step Forward?" O'Daniel, 56–68.

Perry, Patsy Brewington. "*One Day When I Was Lost:* B's Unfulfilled Obligation." O'Daniel, 213–227.

Rosenblatt, Roger. "*Go Tell It on the Mountain,*" "*Another Country.*" *Black Fiction* (Cambridge: Harvard U P, 1974), 36–54, 151–158. Rpt as "Out of Control: *Go Tell It on the Mountain* and *Another Country,*" Bloom.

Rupp, Richard H. "JB: The Search for Celebration." *Celebration in Postwar American Fiction* (Coral Gables: U Miami, P, 1970), 133–149.

Standley, Fred L. "'. . . Farther and Farther Apart': Richard Wright and JB." *Critical Essays on Richard Wright,* ed Yoshinobu Hakutani (Boston: Hall, 1982), 91–103.

Standley. "*Go Tell It on the Mountain:* Religion as the Indirect Method of Indictment." Standley & Burt, 188–194.

Wasserstrom, William. "JB: Stepping Out on the Promise." *Black Fiction,* ed A Robert Lee (NY: Barnes & Noble, 1980), 74–96.

*Williams, Sherley Anne. "The Black Musician: The Black Hero as Light Bearer." *Give Birth to Brightness* (NY: Dial, 1972), 135–166. Rpt Kinnamon.

ARTICLES

Albert, Richard N. "The Jazz-Blues Motif in JB's 'Sonny's Blues.'" *College Literature,* 11 (Spring 1984), 178–185.

*Alexander, Charlotte. "The 'Stink' of Reality: Mothers and Whores in JB's Fiction." *Literature and Psychology,* 18, no 1 (1968), 9–26. Rpt Kinnamon.

*Allen, Shirley S. "Religious Symbolism and Psychic Reality in B's *Go Tell It on the Mountain.*" *College Language Association Journal,* 19 (Dec 1975), 173–199. Rpt Standley & Burt.

Angelou, Maya. "A Brother's Love: JB Remembered." *New York Times Book Review* (20 Dec 1987), 29–30. Rpt Troupe.

*Baker, Houston A, Jr. "The Embattled Craftsman: An Essay on JB." *Journal of African—Afro-American Affairs,* 1 (Jun 1977), 28–51. Rpt Standley & Burt.

Baraka, Amiri. "We Carry Him as Us." *New York Times Book Review* (20 Dec 1987), 27, 29. Rpt as "Jimmy!," Troupe.

Barksdale, Richard K. "Temple of the Fire Baptised." *Phylon,* 14, no 3 (1953), 326–327. Rpt Standley & Burt.

Bawer, Bruce. "Race and Art: The Career of JB." *New Criterion,* 10 (Nov 1991), 16–26.

Bayles, Martha. "JB: On the Tube at Last. . . ." *Wall Street Journal* (14 Jan 1985), 14. Rpt Standley & Burt.

Bell, Pearl K. "Roth and B: Coming Home." *Commentary,* 68 (Dec 1979), 72–75. Rpt Bloom.

Bigsby, C W E. "The Divided Mind of JB." *Journal of American Studies*, 13 (Dec 1979), 325–342. Rpt Bloom, Standley & Burt.

Bluefarb, Sam. "JB's 'Previous Condition': A Problem of Identification." *Negro American Literature Forum*, 3 (Spring 1969), 26–29. Rpt O'Daniel.

Bone, Robert A. "The Novels of JB." *TriQuarterly*, 3 (Winter 1965), 3–20. Rpt *The Negro Novel in America* by Bone (New Haven, Conn: Yale U P, rev 1965). Rpt *Images of the Negro in American Literature*, ed Seymour Gross & John Hardy (Chicago: U Chicago P, 1966). Rpt *The Black Novelist*, ed Robert Hemenway (Columbus, Ohio: Merrill, 1970). Rpt Kinnamon.

Bozkurt, Saadet. "Harmony Within and Without: JB's Quest for Humanity." *American Studies International*, 20 (Autumn 1981), 45–51.

Byerman, Keith E. "Words and Music: Narrative Ambiguity in 'Sonny's Blues.'" *Studies in Short Fiction*, 19 (Fall 1982), 367–372. Rpt Standley & Burt.

Cederstrom, Lorelei. "Love, Race, and Sex in the Novels of JB." *Mosaic*, 17 (Spring 1984), 175–188.

Charney, Maurice. "JB's Quarrel With Richard Wright." *American Quarterly*, 15 (Spring 1963), 65–75. Rpt Gibson.

Clark, Michael. "JB's 'Sonny Blues': Childhood Light and Art." *College Language Association Journal*, 29 (Dec 1985), 197–205.

Clarke, John Henrik. "The Alienation of JB." *Journal of Human Relations*, 12, no 1 (1964), 30–33. Rpt *Harlem U.S.A.* by Clarke (NY: Collier, rev 1971). Rpt *Black Expression*, ed Addison Gayle, Jr (NY: Weybright & Talley, 1969).

Cleaver, Eldridge. "Notes on a Native Son." *Ramparts*, 5 (Jun 1966), 51–52, 54–56. Rpt *Soul on Ice* by Cleaver (NY: Dell, 1968). Rpt *Black Expression*, ed Addison Gayle, Jr (NY: Weybright & Talley, 1969). Rpt *The Black Novelist*, ed Robert Hemenway (Columbus, Ohio: Merrill, 1970). Rpt Kinnamon.

Clurman, Harold. "The Amen Corner." *Nation*, 200 (10 May 1965), 514–515. Rpt Standley & Burt.

Coles, Robert. "B's Burden." *Partisan Review*, 31 (Summer 1964), 409–416.

Collier, Eugenia W. "The Phrase Unbearably Repeated." *Phylon*, 25, no 3 (1964), 288–296. Rpt O'Daniel.

*Collier. "A Study in Chaos." *Black World*, 21 (Jun 1972), 28–34. Rpt as "Thematic Patterns in B's Essays," O'Daniel.

Coombs, Orde. "The Devil Finds Work." *New York Times Book Review* (2 May 1976), 6–7. Rpt Standley & Burt.

Courage, Richard A. "JB's *Go Tell It on the Mountain:* Voices of a People." *College Language Association Journal,* 32 (Jun 1989), 410–425.

*Dance, Daryl C. "You Can't Go Home Again: JB and the South." *College Language Association Journal,* 18 (Sep 1974), 81–90. Rpt Standley & Burt.

DeMott, Benjamin. "JB on the Sixties: Acts and Revelations." *Saturday Review,* 55 (27 May 1972), 63–66. Rpt Kinnamon.

Driver, Tom F. "The Review That Was Too True to Be Published." *Negro Digest,* 13 (Sep 1964), 34–40. Rpt Standley & Burt.

Dupee, F W. "JB and the 'Man.'" *New York Review of Books,* 1 (Special Issue [Feb 1963]), 1–2. Rpt *The King of the Cats and Other Remarks on Writers and Writing* by Dupee (NY: Farrar, Straus & Giroux, second ed 1965), 208–214. Rpt Kinnamon, Bloom.

Ellison, Ralph. "The World and the Jug." *New Leader,* 46 (9 Dec 1963), 22–26. Rpt *Shadow and Act* by Ellison (NY: Random House, 1964).

Fabre, Michel. "Pères et Fils dans *Go Tell It on the Mountain,* de JB." *Etudes Anglaises,* 23 (1970), 47–61. Rpt as "Fathers and Sons in JB's *Go Tell It on the Mountain,*" trans Katherine P Mack. *Modern Black Novelists: A Collection of Critical Essays,* ed M G Cooke (Englewood Cliffs, NJ: Prentice-Hall, 1971). Rpt, trans Kinnamon, Kinnamon.

Featherstone, Joseph. "Blues for Mister B." *New Republic,* 153 (27 Nov 1965), 34–36. Rpt Standley & Burt.

*Fiedler, Leslie A. "A Homosexual Dilemma." *New Leader,* 39 (10 Dec 1956), 16–17. Rpt Standley & Burt.

Gayle, Addison, Jr. "A Defense of JB." *College Language Association Journal,* 10 (Mar 1967), 201–208.

Hagopian, John V. "JB: The Black and the Red-White-and-Blue." *College Language Association Journal,* 7 (Dec 1963), 133–140. Rpt Gibson, O'Daniel.

*Harris, Trudier. "The Eye as Weapon in *If Beale Street Could Talk.*" *MELUS,* 5 (Fall 1978), 54–66. Rpt Standley & Burt.

Howe, Irving. "Black Boys and Native Sons." *Dissent,* 10 (Autumn 1963), 353–368. Rpt *A World More Attractive* by Howe (NY: Horizon, 1963). Rpt *A Casebook on Ralph Ellison's Invisible Man,* ed Joseph F Trimmer (NY: Crowell, 1972).

Howe. "JB: At Ease in Apocalypse." *Harper's,* 237 (Sep 1968), 92, 95–100. Rpt Kinnamon.

Hughes, Langston. "From Harlem to Paris." *New York Times Book Review* (26 Feb 1956), 26. Rpt Kinnamon, Standley & Burt.

Jackson, Jocelyn Whitehead. "The Problem of Identity in Selected Early Essays of JB." *Journal of the Interdenominational Theological Center,* 6 (Fall 1978), 1–15. Rpt Standley & Burt.

*Kent, George E. "B and the Problem of Being." *College Language Association Journal,* 7 (Mar 1964), 202–214. Rpt Gibson, Kinnamon, O'Daniel.

Lash, John S. "B Beside Himself: A Study in Modern Phallicism." *College Language Association Journal,* 8 (Dec 1964), 132–140. Rpt O'Daniel.

*Lester, Julius. "Some Tickets Are Better: The Mixed Achievement of JB." *Dissent,* 33 (Spring 1986), 189–192, 214. Rpt Standley & Burt.

Levin, David. "B's Autobiographical Essays: The Problem of Negro Identity." *Massachusetts Review,* 5 (Winter 1964), 239–247. Rpt *Black & White in American Culture,* ed Jules Chametzky & Sidney Kaplan (Amherst: U Massachusetts P, 1969).

MacInnes, Colin. "Dark Angel: The Writings of JB." *Encounter,* 21 (Aug 1963), 22–33. Rpt Gibson.

May, John R. "Images of Apocalypse in the Black Novel." *Renascence,* 23 (Autumn 1970), 31–45. Rpt as "Ellison, B and Wright: Vestiges of Christian Apocalypse." *Toward a New Earth* by May (Notre Dame, Ind: U Notre Dame P, 1972).

Mayfield, Julian. "A Love Affair With the United States." *New Republic,* 145 (7 Aug 1961), 25. Rpt Standley & Burt.

Moore, John Rees. "An Embarrassment of Riches: B's *Going to Meet the Man.*" *Hollins Critic,* 2 (Dec 1965), 1–12. Rpt *The Sounder Few,* ed R H W Dillard, George Garrett & John R Moore (Athens: U Georgia P, 1971).

Morrison, Toni. "Life in His Language: JB Remembered." *New York Times Book Review* (20 Dec 1987), 27. Rpt Troupe.

Mosher, Marlene. "JB's Blues." *College Language Association Journal,* 26 (Sep 1982), 112–124. Rpt Standley & Burt.

Nelson, Emmanuel S. "JB's Vision of Otherness and Community." *MELUS,* 10, no 2 (1983), 27–31. Rpt Standley & Burt.

Nelson. "The Novels of JB: Struggles of Self-Acceptance." *Journal of American Culture,* 8 (Winter 1985), 11–16.

Newman, Charles. "The Lesson of the Master: Henry James and JB." *Yale Review,* 56 (Oct 1966), 45–59. Rpt Kinnamon, Bloom.

*Oates, Joyce Carol. "A Quite Moving and Very Traditional Celebration of Love." *New York Times Book Review* (26 May 1974), 1–2. Rpt Standley & Burt.

O'Daniel, Therman. "JB: An Interpretive Study." *College Language Association Journal,* 7 (Sep 1963), 37–47.

Pinckney, Darryl. "Blues for Mr. B." *New York Review of Books* (6 Dec 1979), 32–33. Rpt Standley & Burt.

Powers, Lyall H. "Henry James and JB: The Complex Figure." *Modern Fiction Studies,* 30 (Winter 1984), 651–667.

Pratt, Louis H. "JB and 'The Literary Ghetto.'" *College Language Association Journal,* 20 (Dec 1976), 262–272.

*Pratt. "The Political Significance of JB's Early Criticism." *MAWA Review,* 1, no 2–3 (1982), 46–49. Rpt Standley & Burt.

Puzo, Mario. "His Cardboard Lovers." *New York Times Book Review* (23 Jun 1968), 5, 34. Rpt Standley & Burt.

Reilly, John M. "'Sonny's Blues': JB's Image of Black Community." *Negro American Literature Forum,* 4 (Jul 1970), 56–60. Rpt Kinnamon, O'Daniel.

Roth, Philip. "Channel X: Two Plays on the Race Conflict." *New York Review of Books* (28 May 1964), 10–11. Rpt as "Blues for Mister Charlie," Bloom.

Shawcross, John T. "Joy and Sadness: JB, Novelist." *Callaloo,* 6 (Spring–Summer 1983), 100–111.

Snead, James A. "B Looks Back." *Los Angeles Times Book Review* (1 Dec 1985), 1, 6. Rpt Bloom.

Spender, Stephen. "JB: Voice of a Revolution." *Partisan Review,* 30 (Summer 1963), 256–260. Rpt Standley & Burt.

Standley, Fred L. "JB: The Crucial Situation." *South Atlantic Quarterly,* 65 (Summer 1966), 371–381.

*Standley. "JB: The Artist as Incorrigible Disturber of the Peace." *Southern Humanities Review,* 4 (Winter 1970), 18–30. Rpt Standley & Burt.

Standley. "*Another Country:* Another Time:" *Studies in the Novel,* 4 (Fall 1972), 504–512.

Styron, William. "Jimmy's in the House." *New York Times Book Review* (20 Dec 1987), 30. Rpt Troupe.

*Traylor, Eleanor. "I Hear Music in the Air: JB's *Just Above My Head.*" *First World,* 2, no 3 (1979), 40–43. Rpt Standley & Burt, Troupe.

Watkins, Mel. "The Fire Next Time This Time." *New York Times Book Review* (28 May 1972), 17–18. Rpt Standley & Burt.

*Werner, Craig. "The Economic Evolution of JB." *College Language Association Journal,* 23 (Sep 1979), 12–31. Rpt Standley & Burt.

Whitlow, Roger. "B's *Going to Meet the Man:* Racial Brutality and Sexual Gratification." *American Imago,* 34 (Winter 1977), 351–356. Rpt Standley & Burt.

Zahorski, Kenneth J. "A Rap on Race by Margaret Mead and JB." *College Language Association Journal,* 14 (Jun 1971), 470–473. Rpt as "JB: Portrait of a Black Exile," O'Daniel.

— Fred L. Standley

CHARLES WADDELL CHESNUTT

Cleveland, Ohio, 20 Jun 1858–Cleveland, Ohio, 15 Nov 1932

Charles W. Chesnutt is regarded as the first African American writer to achieve artistic success in prose fiction. His short story "The Goophered Grapevine," appearing in the *Atlantic Monthly* of August 1887, presented him to a national literary audience. Nevertheless, the book-buying public at the turn of the century was not eager to read fiction of the color line written from an antiracist perspective. The literary career that began so auspiciously lasted less than twenty years as the discouraged Chesnutt turned to more lucrative business activity and to civic affairs. With the sharply increased interest during recent years in African American literature, Chesnutt has been reassessed and accorded a solid position as a master of the short story, a provocative novelist, a local colorist of fidelity and charm, and a skillful analyst of the social, psychological, and moral results of racism.

Bibliographies

Andrews, William L. "CWC: An Essay in Bibliography." *Resources for American Literary Study,* 6 (Spring 1976), 3–22. Secondary.

Ellison, Curtis W & E W Metcalf, Jr. *CWC: A Reference Guide.* Boston: Hall, 1977. Secondary.

First Printings of American Authors, Vol 3 (Detroit: Bruccoli Clark/Gale, 1978), 47–49. Primary.

Books

The Conjure Woman. Boston & NY: Houghton, Mifflin, 1899. Stories.

Frederick Douglass. Boston: Small, Maynard, 1899. Biography.

The Wife of His Youth and Other Stories of the Color Line. Boston & NY: Houghton, Mifflin, 1899.

The House Behind the Cedars. Boston & NY: Houghton, Mifflin, 1900. Novel.

The Marrow of Tradition. Boston & NY: Houghton, Mifflin, 1901. Novel.

The Colonel's Dream. NY: Doubleday, Page, 1905. Novel.

Baxter's Procrustes. Cleveland: Rowfant Club, 1966. Story.

Collection

The Short Fiction of CWC, ed Sylvia Lyons Render. Washington: Howard U P, 1974.

Manuscripts & Archives

The major collections are at Fisk U Library & Western Reserve Historical Society, Cleveland, Ohio.

Biographies

BOOKS

Chesnutt, Helen M. *CWC: Pioneer of the Color Line.* Chapel Hill: U North Carolina P, 1952.

*Keller, Frances Richardson. *An American Crusade: The Life of CWC.* Provo, Utah: Brigham Young U P, 1978.

Critical Studies

BOOKS

*Andrews, William L. *The Literary Career of CWC.* Baton Rouge: Louisiana State U P, 1980.

Heermance, J Noel. *CWC: America's First Great Black Novelist*. Hamden, Conn: Archon, 1974.

*Render, Sylvia Lyons. *CWC*. Boston: Twayne, 1980.

BOOK SECTIONS

Bender, Bert. "The Lyrical Short Fiction of Dunbar and C." *A Singer in the Dawn: Reinterpretations of Paul Laurence Dunbar,* ed Jay Martin (NY: Dodd, Mead, 1975), 208-222.

*Bone, Robert. "CC." *Down Home: A History of Afro-American Short Fiction From Its Beginnings to the End of the Harlem Renaissance* (NY: Putnam, 1975), 74–105, 293–295.

Elder, Arlene A. "CWC: Art or Assimilation?" *The "Hindered Hand": Cultural Implications of Early African-American Fiction* (Westport, Conn: Greenwood, 1978), 147–197.

Farnsworth, Robert M. "Testing the Color Line—Dunbar and C." *The Black American Writer, Vol I: Fiction,* ed C W E Bigsby (De Land, Fla: Everett/Edwards, 1969), 111–124.

*Farnsworth. "CC and the Color Line." *Minor American Novelists,* ed Charles A Hoyt (Carbondale: Southern Illinois U P, 1970), 28–40, 139.

*Gayle, Addison, Jr. "The Souls of Black Folk." *The Way of the New World: The Black Novel in America* (Garden City, NY: Doubleday, 1975), 25–58, 317–318.

*Gibson, Donald B. "CWC: The Anatomy of a Dream." *The Politics of Literary Expression: A Study of Major Black Writers* (Westport, Conn: Greenwood, 1981), 125–154.

Hathaway, Heather. "'Maybe Freedom Lies in Hating': Miscegenation and the Oedipal Conflict." *Refiguring the Father: New Feminist Readings of Patriarchy,* ed Patricia Yaeger & Beth Kowaleski-Wallace (Carbondale: Southern Illinois U P, 1989), 153–167.

Payne, Ladell. "Trunk and Branch: CWC, 1858–1932." *Black Novelists and the Southern Literary Tradition* (Athens: U Georgia P, 1981), 9–25, 104–106.

*Render, Sylvia Lyons. "Introduction." *The Short Fiction of CWC,* 3–56.

Selke, Hartmut K. "CWC: 'The Sheriff's Children' (1889)." *The Black American Short Story in the 20th Century: A Collection of Critical Essays,* ed Peter Bruck (Amsterdam: Grüner, 1977), 21–38.

*Stepto, Robert B. "'The simple but intensely human life of slavery': Storytelling and the Revision of History in CWC's 'Uncle Julius Stories.'"

History and Tradition in Afro-American Culture, ed Günter H Lenz (Frankfurt: Campus, 1984), 29–55.

Turner, Darwin T. "Introduction." *The House Behind the Cedars* (Riverside, NJ: Collier, 1969), vii–xx.

*Werner, Craig. "The Framing of CWC: Practical Deconstruction in the Afro-American Tradition." *Southern Literature and Literary Theory,* ed Jefferson Humphries (Athens: U Georgia P, 1990), 339–365.

*Wideman, John Edgar. "CC and the WPA Narratives: The Oral and Literate Roots of Afro-American Literature." *The Slave's Narrative,* ed Charles T Davis & Henry Louis Gates, Jr (NY: Oxford U P, 1985), 59–78.

Wilson, Charles E, Jr. "C's 'Baxter's Procrustes': Cultural Fraud as Link to Cultural Identity." *Cultural Power/Cultural Literacy,* ed Bonnie Braendlin (Tallahassee: Florida State U P, 1991), 120–128.

ARTICLES

Ames, Russell. "Social Realism in CWC." *Phylon,* 14, no 2 (1953), 199–206.

Andrews, William L. "C's Patesville: The Presence and Influence of the Past in *The House Behind the Cedars.*" *College Language Association Journal,* 15 (Mar 1972), 284–294.

*Andrews. "William Dean Howells and CWC: Criticism and Race Fiction in the Age of Booker T. Washington." *American Literature,* 48 (Nov 1976), 327–339.

Babb, Valerie. "Subversion and Repatriation in *The Conjure Woman.*" *Southern Quarterly,* 25 (Winter 1987), 66–75.

*Baldwin, Richard E. "The Art of *The Conjure Woman.*" *American Literature,* 43 (Nov 1971), 385–398.

Blake, Susan L. "A Better Mousetrap: Washington's Program and *The Colonel's Dream.*" *College Language Association Journal,* 23 (Sep 1979), 49–59.

Britt, David D. "C's Conjure Tales: What You See Is What You Get." *College Language Association Journal,* 15 (Mar 1972), 269–283.

Burnette, R V. "CWC's *The Conjure Woman* Revisited." *College Language Association Journal,* 30 (Jun 1987), 438–453.

Chametzky, Jules. "Regional Literature and Ethnic Realities." *Antioch Review,* 31 (Fall 1971), 385–396.

Condit, John H. "Pulling a C Out of the Fire: 'Hot-Foot Hannibal.'" *College Language Association Journal,* 30 (Jun 1987), 428–437.

*Delmar, P Jay. "The Mask as Theme and Structure: CWC's 'The Sheriff's Children' and 'The Passing of Grandison.'" *American Literature,* 51 (Nov 1979), 364–375.

Delmar. "Elements of Tragedy in CWC's *The Conjure Woman.*" *College Language Association Journal,* 23 (Jun 1980), 451–459.

Delmar. "Character and Structure in CWC's *The Marrow of Tradition* (1901)." *American Literary Realism,* 13 (Autumn 1980), 284–289.

Delmar. "Coincidence in CWC's *The House Behind the Cedars.*" *American Literary Realism,* 15 (Spring 1982), 97–103.

*Dixon, Melvin. "The Teller as Folk Trickster in C's *The Conjure Woman.*" *College Language Association Journal,* 18 (Dec 1974), 186–197.

Ferguson, SallyAnn H. "C's 'The Conjurer's Revenge': The Economics of Direct Confrontation." *Obsidian,* 7 (Summer–Winter 1981), 37–42.

Ferguson. "Rena Warden: C's Failed 'Future American.'" *Southern Literary Journal,* 15 (Fall 1982), 74–82.

*Fienberg, Lorne. "CWC and Uncle Julius: Black Storytellers at the Crossroads." *Studies in American Fiction,* 15 (Autumn 1987), 161–173.

Fienberg. "CWC's *The Wife of His Youth:* The Unveiling of the Black Storyteller." *American Transcendental Quarterly,* ns 4 (Sep 1990), 219–237.

Fraiman, Susan. "Mother-Daughter Romance in CWC's 'Her Virginia Mammy.'" *Studies in Short Fiction,* 22 (Fall 1985), 443–448.

George, Marjorie & Richard S Pressman. "Confronting the Shadow: Psycho-Political Repression in C's *The Marrow of Tradition.*" *Phylon,* 48, no 4 (1987), 287–298.

Gidden, Nancy Ann. "'The Gray Wolf's Ha'nt': CWC's Intrusive Failure." *College Language Association Journal,* 27 (Jun 1984), 406–410.

Giles, James R & Thomas P Lally. "Allegory in C's *The Marrow of Tradition.*" *Journal of General Education,* 35, no 4 (1984), 259–269.

Gleason, William. "Voices at the Nadir: CC and David Bryant Fulton." *American Literary Realism,* 24 (Spring 1992), 22–41.

Hackenberry, Charles. "Meaning and Models: The Uses of Characterization in C's *The Marrow of Tradition* and 'Mandy Oxendine.'" *American Literary Realism,* 17 (Autumn 1984), 193–202.

Harris, Trudier. "C's Frank Fowler: A Failure of Purpose?" *College Language Association Journal,* 22 (Mar 1979), 215–228.

Haslam, Gerald W. "'The Sheriff's Children': C's Tragic Racial Parable." *Negro American Literature Forum,* 2 (Summer 1968), 21–26.

*Hemenway, Robert. "'Baxter's Procrustes': Irony and Protest." *College Language Association Journal,* 18 (Dec 1974), 172–185.

*Hemenway. "The Function of Folklore in CC's *The Conjure Woman*." *Journal of the Folklore Institute,* 13, no 3 (1976), 283–309.

*Howells, William Dean. "Mr. CWC's Stories." *Atlantic,* 85 (May 1900), 699–701.

*Hurd, Myles Raymond. "Step by Step: Codification and Construction in C's 'The Passing of Grandison.'" *Obsidian II,* 4 (Winter 1989), 78–90.

Jackson, Wendell. "CWC's Outrageous Fortune." *College Language Association Journal,* 20 (Dec 1976), 195–204.

Lewis, Richard O. "Romanticism in the Fiction of CWC: The Influence of Dickens, Scott, Tourgée, and Douglass." *College Language Association Journal,* 26 (Dec 1982), 145–171.

*Mason, Julian D, Jr. "CWC as Southern Author." *Mississippi Quarterly,* 20 (Spring 1967), 77–89.

Myers, Karen Magee. "Mythic Patterns in CWC's *The Conjure Woman* and Ovid's *Metamorphoses*." *Black American Literature Forum,* 13 (Spring 1979), 13–17.

Oden, Gloria C. "C's Conjure as African Survival." *MELUS,* 5 (Spring 1978), 38–48.

Ogunyemi, Chikwenye Okonjo. "The Africanness of *The Conjure Woman* and *Feather Woman of the Jungle*." *Ariel,* 8 (Apr 1977), 17–30.

Patton, Richard J. "Studyin' 'Bout Ole Julius: A Note on CWC's Uncle Julius McAdoo." *American Literary Realism,* 24 (Spring 1992), 72–79.

*Pettis, Joyce. "The Literary Imagination and the Historic Event: C's Use of History in *The Marrow of Tradition*." *South Atlantic Review,* 55 (Nov 1990), 37–48.

*Reilly, John M. "The Dilemma in C's *The Marrow of Tradition*." *Phylon,* 32, no 1 (1971), 31–38.

Sedlack, Robert P. "The Evolution of CC's *The House Behind the Cedars*." *College Language Association Journal,* 19 (Dec 1975), 125–135.

*Selinger, Eric. "Aunts, Uncles, Audience: Genre and Gender in CC's *The Conjure Woman*." *Black American Literature Forum,* 25 (Winter 1991), 665–688.

Sochen, June. "CWC and the Solution to the Race Problem." *Negro American Literature Forum,* 3 (Summer 1969), 52–56.

*Sollors, Werner. "The Goopher in CC's Conjure Tales: Superstition, Ethnicity, and Modern Metamorphoses." *Letterature d'America: Rivista Trimestrale,* 6 (Spring 1985), 107–129.

Taxel, Joel. "CWC's Sambo: Myth and Reality." *Negro American Literature Forum,* 9 (Winter 1975), 105–108.

Terry, Eugene. "CWC: A Victim of the Color Line." *Contributions to Black Studies,* 1 (1977), 15–44.

Terry. "The Shadow of Slavery in CC's *The Conjure Woman.*" *Ethnic Groups,* 4 (May 1982), 103–125.

Whitt, Lena M. "C's Chinquapin County." *Southern Literary Journal,* 13 (Spring 1981), 41–58.

*Wideman, John Edgar. "CWC: *The Marrow of Tradition.*" *American Scholar,* 42 (Winter 1972–1973), 128–134.

Wintz, Cary D. "Race and Realism in the Fiction of CWC." *Ohio History,* 81 (Spring 1972), 122–130.

— Keneth Kinnamon

RALPH ELLISON
Oklahoma City, Okla, 1 Mar 1914–

Ralph Waldo Ellison has published many essays and several short stories, but only one novel—for which he is principally known. *Invisible Man,* which portrays the symbolic misadventures of a black youth as he moves from the South to the North and then underground, is generally considered a major achievement in both African American and world literature. A *Book Week* poll in 1965 of two hundred writers and critics proclaimed *Invisible Man* the most distinguished work published since World War II.

Bibliographies

Covo, Jacqueline. *The Blinking Eye: RWE and His American, French, German, and Italian Critics, 1952–1971: Bibliographic Essays and a Checklist.* Metuchen, NJ: Scarecrow, 1974. Secondary.

Giza, Joanne. "RE." *Black American Writers: Bibliographical Essays,* Vol 2, ed M Thomas Inge, Maurice Duke & Jackson R Bryer (NY: St Martin, 1978), 47–71. Secondary.

*O'Meally, Robert G. "The Writings of RE." Benston, 411–419. Primary.

Weixlmann, Joe & John O'Banion. "A Checklist of E Criticism, 1972–1978." *Black American Literature Forum,* 12 (Summer 1978), 51–55. Secondary.

Books

Invisible Man. NY: Random House, 1952. Repub with intro by RE, 1982. Novel.

Shadow and Act. NY: Random House, 1964. Essays.

The Writer's Experience: RE and Karl Shapiro. Washington: Library of Congress, 1964. Lecture.

Going to the Territory. NY: Random House, 1986. Essays.

Manuscripts & Archives

Fisk U Library.

Biographies

BOOK

*Bishop, Jack. *RE.* NY: Chelsea House, 1988.

BOOK SECTION

Kostelanetz, Richard. "RE: Novelist as Brown-Skinned Aristocrat." *Master Minds* (NY: Macmillan, 1969), 36–59.

ARTICLES

*Anderson, Jervis. "Going to the Territory." *New Yorker,* 52 (22 Nov 1976), 55–56, 59–60, 62–64, 66, 69–70, 72, 74, 76, 81–82, 84, 86, 88, 91–92, 94, 96, 100–102, 104–105, 108.

Corry, John. "An American Novelist Who Sometimes Teaches." *New York Times Magazine* (20 Nov 1966), 54–55, 179–185, 187, 196. Rpt *Black World,* 20 (Dec 1970), 116–125.

Interviews

BOOK SECTIONS

Graham, John. "RE." *The Writer's Voice,* ed George Garrett (NY: Morrow, 1973), 221–227.

*Hersey, John. "Introduction: A Completion of Personality: A Talk With R.E." Hersey 1–9. Augmented Benston.

O'Brien, John. "RE." *Interviews With Black Writers* (NY: Liveright, 1973), 62–77.

Warren, Robert Penn. "Leadership From the Periphery—no 7." *Who Speaks for the Negro?* (NY: Random House, 1965), 325–354.

ARTICLES

Cannon, Steve, Lennox Raphael & James Thompson. "A Very Stern Discipline." *Harper's*, 234 (Mar 1967), 76–80, 83–86, 88, 90, 93–95.

Carson, David L. "RE: Twenty Years After." *Studies in American Fiction*, 1 (Spring 1973), 1–23.

*Chester, Alfred & Vilma Howard. "The Art of Fiction VIII: RE." *Paris Review*, 3 (Spring 1955), 54–71. Rpt *Writers at Work, Second Series*, ed George Plimpton (NY: Viking, 1963). Rpt *Shadow and Act*. Rpt *The Black Novelist*, ed Robert Hemenway (Columbus, Ohio: Merrill, 1970). Rpt Gottesman.

Geller, Allen. "An Interview With RE." *Tamarack Review*, 32 (Summer 1964), 3–24. Rpt *The Black American Writer*, Vol 1, ed C W E Bigsby (De Land, Fla: Everett/Edwards, 1969).

Harper, Michael S & Robert B Stepto. "Study & Experience: An Interview With RE." *Massachusetts Review*, 18 (Autumn 1977), 417–435. Rpt *Chant of Saints* by Harper & Stepto (Urbana: U Illinois P, 1979).

*McPherson, James Alan. "Indivisible Man." *Atlantic*, 226 (Dec 1970), 45–60. Rpt Hersey.

Critical Studies

BOOKS

List, Robert N. *Dedalus in Harlem: The Joyce-E Connection.* Washington: U P America, 1982.

Lynch, Michael F. *Creative Revolt: A Study of Wright, E, and Dostoevsky.* NY: Lang, 1990.

*McSweeney, Kerry. *Invisible Man: Race and Identity.* Boston: Twayne, 1988.

Nadel, Alan. *Invisible Criticism: RE and the American Canon.* Iowa City: U Iowa P, 41988.

*O'Meally, Robert G. *The Craft of RE.* Cambridge, Mass: Harvard U P, 1980.

COLLECTIONS OF ESSAYS

*Benston, Kimberly W, ed. *Speaking for You: The Vision of RE.* Washington: Howard U P, 1987.

*Bloom, Harold, ed. *RE: Modern Critical Views.* NY: Chelsea House, 1986.

Gottesman, Ronald, ed. *Merrill Studies in Invisible Man.* Columbus, Ohio: Merrill, 1971.

*Hersey, John, ed. *RE: A Collection of Critical Essays.* Englewood Cliffs, NJ: Prentice-Hall, 1974.

*O'Meally, Robert, ed. *New Essays on Invisible Man.* Cambridge: Cambridge U P, 1988.

*Parr, Susan Resneck & Pancho Savery, eds. *Approaches to Teaching E's Invisible Man.* NY: MLA, 1989.

Reilly, John M, ed. *Twentieth-Century Interpretations of Invisible Man: A Collection of Critical Essays.* Englewood Cliffs, NJ: Prentice-Hall, 1970.

Trimmer, Joseph F, ed. *A Casebook on RE's Invisible Man.* NY: Crowell, 1972.

SPECIAL JOURNALS

Black World, 20 (Dec 1970). RE issue.

College Language Association Journal, 13 (Mar 1970). RE issue.

Carleton Miscellany, 18 (Winter 1980). RE issue.

BOOK SECTIONS

Alexander, Sandra Carlton. "The Scapegoat Archetype in RE's *Invisible Man.*" *Afro-American Folklore,* ed George E Carter & James R Parker (La Crosse: U Wisconsin, 1977), 31–38.

Allen, Michael. "Some Examples of Faulknerian Rhetoric in E's *Invisible Man.*" *The Black American Writer,* Vol 1, ed C W F. Bigsby (De Land, Fla: Everett/Edwards, 1969), 143–151.

*Baumbach, Jonathan. "Nightmare of a Native Son: *Invisible Man* by RE." *The Landscape of Nightmare* (NY: NYU P, 1965), 68–86. Rpt *Five Black Writers,* ed Donald B Gibson (NY: NYU P, 1970). Rpt Bloom.

Bell, Bernard W. "RWE." *The Afro-American Novel and Its Tradition* (Amherst: U Massachusetts P, 1987), 193–215.

Benston, Kimberly W. "The Masks of RE." Benston, 3–8.

Bigsby, C W E. "The Flight of Words: The Paradox of RE." *The Second Black Renaissance,* ed Bigsby (Westport, Conn: Greenwood, 1980), 85–104.

Bigsby. "Improvising America: RE and the Paradox of Form." Benston, 173–183.

Bone, Robert A. "The Contemporary Negro Novel." *The Negro Novel in America* (New Haven, Conn: Yale U P, rev 1965), 173–212.

*Bone. "RE and the Uses of the Imagination." *Anger and Beyond,* ed Herbert Hill (NY: Harper & Row, 1966), 86–111. Rpt Reilly, Gottesman, Trimmer, Hersey.

Burke, Kenneth. "RE's Trueblood *Bildungsroman.*" Benston, 349–359.

Byerman, Keith E. "History Against History: A Dialectical Pattern in *Invisible Man.*" *Fingering the Jagged Grain* (Athens: U Georgia P, 1985), 11–40.

*Callahan, John F. "The Historical Frequencies of RWE." *Chant of Saints,* ed Michael S Harper & Robert B Stepto (Urbana: U Illinois P, 1979), 33–52. Rpt Benston.

Callahan. "Frequencies of Eloquence: The Performance and Composition of *Invisible Man.*" O'Meally, 55–94.

Campbell, Jane. "Retreat into the Self: RE's *Invisible Man* and James Baldwin's *Go Tell It on the Mountain.*" *Mythic Black Fiction* (Knoxville: U Tennessee P, 1986), 87–110.

Christian, Barbara. "RE: A Critical Study." *Black Expression,* ed Addison Gayle, Jr (NY: Weybright & Talley, 1969), 353–365.

Cooke, Michael G. "Solitude: The Beginning of Self-Realization in Zora Neale Hurston, Richard Wright, and RE." *Afro-American Literature in the Twentieth Century* (New Haven, Conn: Yale U P, 1984), 71–109. Rpt Bloom.

Davis, Arthur P. "RE." *From the Dark Tower* (Washington: Howard U P, 1974), 207–216.

Davis, Charles T. "The Mixed Heritage of the Modern Black Novel: RE and Friends." *Black Is the Color of the Cosmos,* ed Henry Louis Gates, Jr (NY: Garland, 1982), 313–325. Rpt Benston.

Dietze, Rudolf F. "RE and the Literary Tradition." *History and Tradition in Afro-American Culture,* ed Günter H Lenz (Frankfurt, Germany: Campus Verlag, 1984), 118–129.

Gayle, Addison, Jr. "Of Race and Rage." *The Way of the New World* (Garden City, NY: Doubleday, 1975), 203–220.

Gibson, Donald B. "RE and James Baldwin." *The Politics of Twentieth-Century Novelists,* ed George A Panichas (NY: Hawthorn, 1971), 307–320.

Gibson. "RE's *Invisible Man:* The Politics of Retreat." *The Politics of Literary Expression* (Westport, Conn: Greenwood, 1981), 59–98.

Guttmann, Allen. "Focus on RE's *Invisible Man:* American Nightmare." *American Dreams, American Nightmares,* ed David Madden (Carbondale: Southern Illinois U P, 1970), 188–196.

Holland, Laurence B. "E in Black and White: Confession, Violence and Rhetoric in *Invisible Man.*" *Black Fiction,* ed A Robert Lee (NY: Harper & Row, 1980), 54–73.

*Horowitz, Ellin. "The Rebirth of the Artist." *On Contemporary Literature,* ed Richard Kostelanetz (NY: Avon, 1964), 330–346. Rpt Reilly, Trimmer.

*Howe, Irving. "Black Boys and Native Sons." *A World More Attractive* (NY: Horizon, 1963), 98–122. Rpt Trimmer, Hersey.

*Klein, Marcus. "RE." *After Alienation* (Cleveland, Ohio: World, 1964), 71–146. Rpt as "RE's *Invisible Man,*" *Five Black Writers,* ed Donald B Gibson (NY: NYU P / London: U London P, 1970). Rpt as "RE's *Invisible Man,*" Gottesman.

Lee, A Robert. "Harlem on My Mind: Fictions of a Black Metropolis." *The American City: Literary and Cultural Perspectives,* ed Graham Clarke (London: Vision/NY: St Martin, 1988), 62–85.

Margolies, Edward. "History as Blues: RE's *Invisible Man.*" *Native Sons* (Philadelphia: Lippincott, 1968), 127–148.

Mueller, William R. "RE: A Portrait of the Artist as a Young Man." *Celebration of Life* (NY: Sheed & Ward, 1972), 50–68.

Murray, Albert. "Something Different, Something More." *Anger, and Beyond,* ed Herbert Hill (NY: Harper & Row, 1966), 112–137.

O'Meally, Robert G. "Riffs and Rituals: Folklore in the World of RE." *Afro-American Literature,* ed Dexter Fisher & Robert B Stepto (NY: MLA, 1979), 153–169.

Ostendorf, Berndt. "Anthropology, Modernism, and Jazz." Bloom, 145–172. Rpt O'Meally.

Payne, Ladell. "The Shadow of the Past: RE 1914—." *Black Novelists and the Southern Literary Tradition* (Athens: U Georgia P, 1981), 80–98.

Real, Willi. "RE: 'King of the Bingo Game.'" *The Black American Short Story in the 20th Century,* ed Peter Bruck (Amsterdam: Grüner, 1977), 111–127.

Reilly, John M. "The Testament of RE." Benston, 49–62.

*Robinson, Douglas. "Call Me Jonah." *American Apocalypses* (Baltimore, Md: Johns Hopkins U P, 1985), 125–162. Rpt Bloom.

Smith, Valerie. "E's Invisible Autobiographer." *Self-Discovery and Authority in Afro-American Narrative* (Cambridge: Harvard U P, 1987), 88–121.

Smith. "The Meaning of Narration in *Invisible Man*." O'Meally, 25–53.

Spillers, Hortense J. "'The Permanent Obliquity of an In(pha)llibly Straight': In the Time of the Daughters and the Fathers." *Changing Our Own Words: Essays on Criticism, Theory, and Writing by Black Women,* ed Cheryl A Wall (New Brunswick, NJ: Rutgers U P, 1989), 127–149.

*Stepto, Robert B. "Literacy and Hibernation: RE's *Invisible Man*." *From Behind the Veil* (Urbana: U Illinois P, 1979), 163–194. Rpt *Carleton Miscellany,* 18 (Winter 1980), 112–141. Rpt Bloom, Benston.

*Tanner, Tony. "The Music of Invisibility." *City of Words* (NY: Harper & Row, 1971), 50–63. Rpt Hersey, Bloom.

Tate, Claudia. "Notes on the Invisible Women in RE's *Invisible Man*." Benston, 163–172.

Urgo, Joseph R. "Contemplating the Unthinkable: The Myth of Racial Existence in RE's America." *Novel Frames: Literature as Guide to Race, Sex, and History in American Culture* (Jackson: U P Mississippi, 1991), 5–37.

Wright, Austin M. "Rhetorical Plot: *Invisible Man*." *The Formal Principle in the Novel* (Ithaca, NY: Cornell U P, 1982), 240–259.

Wright, John S. "The Conscious Hero and the Rites of Man: E's War." O'Meally, 157–186.

Wright. "To the Battle Royal: RE and the Quest for Black Leadership in Postwar America." *Recasting America: Culture and Politics in the Age of the Cold War,* ed Lary May (Chicago: U Chicago P, 1989), 246–266.

ARTICLES

*Abrams, Robert E. "The Ambiguities of Dreaming in E's *Invisible Man*." *American Literature,* 49 (Jan 1978), 592–603.

Baker, Houston A, Jr. "A Forgotten Prototype: *The Autobiography of an Ex-Colored Man* and *Invisible Man*." *Virginia Quarterly Review,* 49 (Summer 1973), 433–449. Rpt *Singers of Daybreak* by Baker (Washington: Howard U P, 1974).

*Baker. "To Move Without Moving: An Analysis of Creativity and Commerce in RE's 'Trueblood Episode.'" *PMLA,* 98 (Oct 1983), 828–845. Rpt as "A Dream of American Form," *Blues, Ideology, and Afro-American Literature* by Baker (Chicago: U Chicago P, 1984). Excerpted as "Creativity and Commerce in RE's 'Trueblood Episode,'" Bloom. Rpt as "To Move Without Moving: An Analysis of Creativity and Commerce in RE's 'Trueblood Episode,'" Benston.

Bellow, Saul. "Man Underground." *Commentary*, 13 (Jun 1952), 608–610. Rpt Hersey.

*Bennett, Stephen B & William W Nichols. "Violence in Afro-American Fiction: An Hypothesis." *Modern Fiction Studies*, 17 (Summer 1971), 221–228. Rpt Hersey.

Benston, Kimberly W. "E, Baraka, and the Faces of Tradition." *Boundary 2*, 6 (Winter 1978), 333–354.

*Blake, Susan L. "Ritual and Rationalization: Black Folklore in the Works of RE." *PMLA*, 94 (Jan 1979), 121–136. Rpt Bloom.

Bloch, Alice. "Sight Imagery in *Invisible Man*." *English Journal*, 55 (Nov 1966), 1019–1021, 1024. Rpt Trimmer.

Bluestein, Gene. "The Blues as a Literary Theme." *Massachusetts Review*, 8 (Autumn 1967), 593–617.

Brennan, Timothy. "E and E: The Solipsism of *Invisible Man*." *College Language Association Journal*, 25 (Dec 1981), 162–181.

Brown, Lloyd W. "RE's Exhorters: The Role of Rhetoric in *Invisible Man*." *College Language Association Journal*, 13 (Mar 1970), 289–303.

Bryant, Jerry H. "Wright, E, Baldwin—Exorcising the Demon." *Phylon*, 37 (Jun 1976), 174–188.

Bucco, Martin. "E's Invisible West." *Western American Literature*, 10 (Fall 1975), 237–238.

Butler, Robert J. "Patterns of Movement in E's *Invisible Man*." *American Studies*, 21 (Spring 1980), 5–21.

Butler. "Dante's *Inferno* and E's *Invisible Man*: A Study in Literary Continuity." *College Language Association Journal*, 28 (Sep 1984), 57–77.

*Butler. "Down From Slavery: Invisible Man's Descent into the City and the Discovery of Self." *American Studies*, 29 (Fall 1988), 57–67.

Butler, Thorpe. "What Is to Be Done? Illusion, Identity, and Action in RE's *Invisible Man*." *College Language Association Journal*, 27 (Mar 1984), 315–331.

*Callahan, John F. "Democracy and the Pursuit of Narrative." *Carleton Miscellany*, 18 (Winter 1980), 51–68.

Callahan. "'Riffing' and Paradigm-Building: The Anomaly of Tradition and Innovation in *Invisible Man* and the Structure of Scientific Revolutions." *Callaloo*, 10 (Winter 1987), 91–102.

Cheshire, Ardner R, Jr. "*Invisible Man* and the Life of Dialogue." *College Language Association Journal*, 20 (Sep 1976), 19–34.

Chisolm, Lawrence Washington. "Signifying Everything." *Yale Review*, 54 (Spring 1965), 450–454. Rpt Hersey.

Clipper, Lawrence J. "Folkloric and Mythic Elements in *Invisible Man.*" *College Language Association Journal,* 13 (Mar 1970), 229–241.

Deutsch, Leonard J. "RWE and Ralph Waldo Emerson: A Shared Moral Vision." *College Language Association Journal,* 16 (Dec 1972), 159–178.

Doyle, Mary Ellen. "In Need of Folk: The Alienated Protagonists of RE's Short Fiction." *College Language Association Journal,* 19 (Dec 1975), 165–172.

Dressel, Janice Hartwick. "The Legacy of RE in Virginia Hamilton's Justice Trilogy." *English Journal,* 73 (Nov 1984), 42–48.

Fabre, Michel. "The Narrator/Narratee Relationship in *Invisible Man.*" *Callaloo,* 8 (Fall 1985), 535–543.

Fass, Barbara. "Rejection of Paternalism: Hawthorne's 'My Kinsman Major Molineux' and E's *Invisible Man.*" *College Language Association Journal,* 14 (Mar 1971), 317–323.

Fischer, Russell G. "*Invisible Man* as History." *College Language Association Journal,* 17 (Mar 1974), 338–367.

Fleming, Robert E. "E's Black Archetypes: The Founder, Bledsoe, Ras, and Rinehart." *College Language Association Journal,* 32 (Jun 1989), 426–432.

Foster, Frances S. "The Black and White Masks of Frantz Fanon and RE." *Black Academy Review,* 1 (Winter 1970), 46–58.

Fraiberg, Selma. "Two Modern Incest Heroes." *Partisan Review,* 28, no 5–6 (1961), 646–661. Rpt Reilly.

German, Norman. "Imagery in the 'Battle Royal' Chapter of RE's *Invisible Man.*" *College Language Association Journal,* 31 (Jun 1988), 394–399.

Glicksberg, Charles. "The Symbolism of Vision." *Southwest Review,* 39 (Summer 1954), 259–265. Rpt Reilly.

Goede, William. "On Lower Frequencies: The Buried Men in Wright and E." *Modern Fiction Studies,* 15 (Winter 1969–1970), 483–501.

Gordon, Gerald T. "Rhetorical Strategy in RE's *Invisible Man.*" *Rocky Mountain Review,* 41, no 4 (1987), 199–210.

Gottschalk, Jane. "Sophisticated Jokes: The Use of American Authors in *Invisible Man.*" *Renascence,* 30 (Winter 1978), 69–77.

Greene, Maxine. "Against Invisibility." *College English,* 30 (Mar 1969), 430–436.

Griffin, Edward M. "Notes From a Clean, Well-Lighted Place: RE's *Invisible Man.*" *Twentieth Century Literature,* 15 (Oct 1969), 129–144.

Grow, Lynn M. "The Dream Scenes of *Invisible Man.*" *Wichita State University Bulletin,* 50, no 3 (1974), 3–13.

Hansen, J T. "A Holistic Approach to *Invisible Man.*" *MELUS,* 6 (Spring 1979), 41–54.

Harper, Phillip Brian. "'To Become One and Yet Many': Psychic Fragmentation and Aesthetic Synthesis in RE's *Invisible Man.*" *Black American Literature Forum,* 23 (Winter 1989), 681–700.

Harris, Trudier. "E's 'Peter Wheatstraw': His Basis in Black Folk Tradition." *Mississippi Folklore Register,* 9 (Summer 1975), 117–126.

Haupt, Garry. "The Tragi-Comedy of the Unreal in RE's *Invisible Man* and Mark Twain's *Adventures of Huckleberry Finn.*" *Interpretations,* 4, no 1 (1972), 1–12.

Helmling, Steven. "T. S. Eliot and RE: Insiders, Outsiders, and Cultural Authority." *Southern Review,* 25 (Autumn 1989), 841–858.

*Horowitz, Floyd R. "RE's Modern Version of Brer Bear and Brer Rabbit in *Invisible Man.*" *Midcontinent American Studies Journal,* 4 (Fall 1963), 21–27. Rpt Reilly, Gottesman, Trimmer.

Howe, Irving. "A Reply to RE." *New Leader,* 47 (3 Feb 1964), 12–22.

Hyman, Stanley Edgar. "RE in Our Time." *New Leader,* 47 (26 Oct 1964), 20–21. Rpt. Reilly, Hersey.

Isaacs, Harold S. "Five Black Writers and Their African Ancestors." *Phylon,* 21 (Winter 1960), 317–336.

Jackson, Esther Merle. "The American Negro and the Image of the Absurd." *Phylon,* 23 (Winter 1962), 359–371. Rpt Reilly.

Johnson, Abby Arthur. "Birds of Passage: Flight Imagery in *Invisible Man.*" *Studies in the Twentieth Century,* no 14 (Fall 1974), 91–104.

*Kent, George E. "RE and the Afro-American Folk and Cultural Tradition." *College Language Association Journal,* 13 (Mar 1970), 265–276. Rpt Hersey, Benston.

*Kostelanetz, Richard. "The Politics of E's Booker: *Invisible Man* as Symbolic History." *Chicago Review,* 19, no 2 (1967), 5–26. Rpt *The Black Novelist* by Robert Hemenway (Columbus, Ohio: Merrill, 1970). Rpt Trimmer.

Lee, A Robert. "Sight and Mask: RE's *Invisible Man.*" *Negro American Literature Forum,* 4 (Mar 1970), 22–33.

Lee, L L. "The Proper Self: RE's *Invisible Man.*" *Descant,* 10 (Spring 1966), 38–48.

*Lehan, Richard. "The Strange Silence of RE." *California English Journal,* 1 (Spring 1965), 63–68. Rpt Reilly.

Lewis, R W B. "E's Essays." *New York Review of Books* (28 Jan 1965), 19–20. Rpt Bloom.

Lieber, Todd M. "RE and the Metaphor of Invisibility in Black Literary Tradition." *American Quarterly,* 24 (Mar 1972), 86–100.

Lieberman, Marcia R. "Moral Innocents: E's *Invisible Man* and *Candide.*" *College Language Association Journal,* 15 (Sep 1971), 64–79.

List, Robert E. "An Object-Relations Approach to E's 'King of the Bingo Game.'" *Researcher,* 13 (Spring 1990), 15–32.

Lyons, Eleanor. "E and the Twentieth-Century American Scholar." *Studies in American Fiction,* 17 (Spring 1989), 93–106.

Marmorstein, Gary. "RE's Not-So-New Novel." *Obsidian,* 6 (Winter 1980), 7–21.

Martin, Mike W. "*Invisible Man* and the Indictment of Innocence." *College Language Association Journal,* 25 (Mar 1982), 288–302.

Marx, Steven. "Beyond Hibernation: RE's 1982 Version of *Invisible Man.*" *Black American Literature Forum,* 23 (Winter 1989), 701–721.

Miyashita, Masatoshi. "An Introduction to the American Plot of Self-(Re)Naming." *Language and Culture,* no 17 (1989), 177–194.

Nash, Russell W. "Stereotypes and Social Types in E's *Invisible Man.*" *Sociological Quarterly,* 6 (Autumn 1965), 349–360.

*Neal, Larry. "Politics as Ritual: E's Zoot Suit." *Black World,* 20 (Dec 1970), 31–52. Rpt as "E's Zoot Suit," Hersey. Rpt as "Politics as Ritual: E's Zoot Suit," Benston.

O'Connor, Eugene & Kenneth W Goings. "My Name Is 'Nobody': African-American and Classic Models of the Trickster in RE's *Invisible Man.*" *Literature Interpretation Theory,* 1 (Mar 1990), 217–227.

*O'Daniel, Therman B. "The Image of Man as Portrayed by RE." *College Language Association Journal,* 10 (Jun 1967), 277–284. Rpt *Five Black Writers,* ed Donald B Gibson (NY: NYU P, 1970). Rpt Reilly.

Ogbaa, Kalu. "Protest and the Individual Talents of Three Black Novelists." *College Language Association Journal,* 35 (Dec 1991), 159–184.

Ogunyemi, Chikwenye Okonjo. "The Old Order Shall Pass: The Examples of 'Flying Home' and 'Barbados.'" *College Language Association Journal,* 25 (Mar 1982), 303–314.

Olderman, Raymond M. "RE's Blues and *Invisible Man.*" *Wisconsin Studies in Contemporary Literature,* 7 (Summer 1966), 142–159.

Oliver, M Celeste. "*Invisible Man* and the Numbers Game." *College Language Association Journal,* 22 (Dec 1978), 123–133.

Omans, Stuart E. "The Variations on a Masked Leader: A Study on the Literary Relationship of RE and Herman Melville." *South Atlantic Bulletin,* 40 (May 1975), 15–23.

*Pryse, Marjorie. "RE's Heroic Fugitive." *American Literature,* 46 (Mar 1974), 1–15.

Rodnon, Stewart. "*The Adventures of Huckleberry Finn* and *Invisible Man:* Thematic and Structural Comparisons." *Negro American Literature Forum,* 4 (Jul 1970), 45–51.

*Rovit, Earl H. "E and the American Comic Tradition." *Wisconsin Studies in Contemporary Literature,* 1 (Fall 1960), 34–42. Rpt *Five Black Writers,* ed Donald B Gibson (NY: NYU P, 1970). Rpt Reilly, Trimmer.

Sadler, Lynn Veach. "RE and the Bird-Artist." *South Atlantic Bulletin,* 44 (Nov 1979), 20–30.

Sanders, Archie D. "Odysseus in Black: An Analysis of the Structure of *Invisible Man.*" *College Language Association Journal,* 13 (Mar 1970), 217–228.

Saunders, Catherine E. "Makers or Bearers of Meaning? Sex and the Struggle for Self-Definition in RE's *Invisible Man.*" *Critical Mattrix,* 5 (Fall–Winter 1989), 1–28.

*Schafer, William J. "RE and the Birth of the Anti-Hero." *Critique,* 10, no 2 (1968), 81–93. Rpt Gottesman, Trimmer, Hersey.

Schafer. "Irony From Underground—Satiric Elements in *Invisible Man.*" *Satire Newsletter,* 7 (Fall 1969), 22–29. Rpt Reilly.

Schor, Edith. "RE, Journeyman: Three Early Stories." *MELUS,* 15 (Summer 1988), 57–69.

Schultz, Elizabeth A. "The Heirs of RE: Patterns of Individualism in the Contemporary Afro-American Novel." *College Language Association Journal,* 22 (Dec 1978), 101–122.

Schultz. "The Illumination of Darkness: Affinities Between *Moby-Dick* and *Invisible Man.*" *College Language Association Journal,* 32 (Dec 1988), 170–200.

Scott, Nathan A, Jr. "E's Vision of *Communitas.*" *Carleton Miscellany,* 18 (Winter 1980), 41–50. Rpt *American Writing Today,* ed Richard Kostelanetz (Troy, NY: Whitson, rev 1991).

Scruggs, Charles W. "RE's Use of *The Aeneid* in *Invisible Man.*" *College Language Association Journal,* 17 (Mar 1974), 368–378.

Singleton, M K. "Leadership Mirages as Antagonists in *Invisible Man.*" *Arizona Quarterly,* 22 (Summer 1966), 157–171. Rpt Reilly.

Stanford, Raney. "The Return of the Trickster: When a Not-A-Hero Is a Hero." *Journal of Popular Culture,* 1 (Winter 1967), 228–242.

Steele, Shelby. "RE's Blues." *Journal of Black Studies,* 7 (Dec 1976), 151–168.

Tewarie, Bhoendradatt. "Southern Elements in E's *Invisible Man.*" *Journal of General Education,* 35, no 3 (1983), 189–200.

Thomas, Gillian & Michael Larsen. "RE's Conjure Doctors." *English Language Notes,* 17 (Jun 1980), 281–288.

Tischler, Nancy M. "Negro Literature and Classic Form." *Contemporary Literature,* 10 (Summer 1969), 352–365.

Tracy, Steven C. "The Devil's Son-in-Law and *Invisible Man.*" *MELUS,* 15 (Fall 1988), 47–64.

Trimmer, Joseph F. "RE's 'Flying Home.'" *Studies in Short Fiction,* 9 (Spring 1972), 175–182.

*Vogler, Thomas A. "*Invisible Man:* Somebody's Protest Novel." *Iowa Review,* 1 (Spring 1970), 64–82. Rpt Gottesman, Hersey.

Walling, William. "'Art' and 'Protest': RE's *Invisible Man* Twenty Years After." *Phylon,* 34 (Jun 1973), 120–134.

Walsh, Mary Ellen Williams. "*Invisible Man:* RE's Wasteland." *College Language Association Journal,* 28 (Dec 1984), 150–158.

Warren, Robert Penn. "The Unity of Experience." *Commentary,* 39 (May 1965), 91–96. Rpt Hersey.

Wasserman, Jerry. "Embracing the Negative: *Native Son* and *Invisible Man.*" *Studies in American Fiction,* 4 (Spring 1976), 93–104.

Weber, Daniel B. "Metropolitan Freedom and Restraint in E's *Invisible Man.*" *College Literature,* 12 (Spring 1985), 163–175.

Winther, Per. "The Ending of RE's *Invisible Man.*" *College Language Association Journal,* 25 (Mar 1982), 267–287.

Wynter, Sylvia. "On Disenchanting Discourse: 'Minority' Literary Criticism and Beyond." *Cultural Critique,* no 7 (Fall 1987), 207–244.

— Leonard J. Deutsch

ZORA NEALE HURSTON

Eatonville, Fla, 7 Jan 1901?–Fort Pierce, Fla, 28 Jan 1960

Zora Neale Hurston, anthropologist, folklorist, and fiction writer, was the most prolific black woman author in the 1930s and 1940s. Initial critical reactions to Hurston's works were mixed: they were praised for their realistic black dialect and folklore, but faulted for a lack of fully developed characters and plots and an absence of racial consciousness. Hurston's books were out of print when she died in poverty and obscurity. In the 1960s and 1970s, however, interest in her writing revived, and critics began to study her stories apart from racial considerations. *Their Eyes Were Watching God* is considered her finest novel in its portrayal of a black woman's quest for identity and fulfillment. Hurston's importance lies not only in her ability to use black culture to write stories with universal concerns but also in her influence on other writers.

Bibliographies

*Dance, Daryl C. "ZNH." *American Women Writers: Bibliographical Essays,* ed Maurice Duke, Jackson R Bryer & M Thomas Inge (Westport, Conn: Greenwood, 1983), 321–351. Primary & secondary.

*Dandridge, Rita B. "On the Novels Written by Selected Black Women: A Bibliographic Essay." *But Some of Us Are Brave,* ed Gloria T Hull, Patricia Bell Scott & Barbara Smith (Old Westbury, NY: Feminist, 1982), 261–279. Primary & secondary.

*Newson, Adele S. *ZNH: A Reference Guide.* Boston: Hall, 1987. Secondary.

Ryan, Bonnie Crarey. "ZNH—A Checklist of Secondary Sources." *Bulletin of Bibliography,* 45 (Mar 1988), 33–39.

Books

Jonah's Gourd Vine. Philadelphia & London: Lippincott, 1934. Novel.

Mules & Men. Philadephia & London: Lippincott, 1935. Folklore.

Their Eyes Were Watching God. Philadelphia & London: Lippincott, 1937. Novel.

Tell My Horse. Philadelphia & c: Lippincott, 1938; *Voodoo Gods: An Inquiry into Native Myths and Magic in Jamaica and Haiti.* London: Dent, 1939. Anthropology & folklore.

Moses: Man of the Mountain. Philadelphia, Pa: Lippincott, 1939; *The Man of the Mountain.* London: Dent, 1941. Novel.

Dust Tracks on a Road: An Autobiography. Philadelphia: Lippincott, 1942.

Seraph on the Suwanee. NY: Scribners, 1948. Novel.

The Sanctified Church. Berkeley, Calif: Turtle Island, 1981. Essays.

Spunk: The Selected Stories of ZNH, foreword by Bob Callahan. Berkeley, Calif: Turtle Island, 1985.

Other

"Hoodo in America." *Journal of American Folklore,* 44 (Oct–Dec 1931), 317–417. Essay.

Caribbean Melodies for Chorus of Mixed Voices and Soloists, collected & annotated by ZNH; music arranged by William Grant Still. Philadelphia, Pa: Ditson, 1947.

Collection

I Love Myself When I Am Laughing . . . And Then Again When I Am Looking Mean and Impressive: A ZNH Reader, ed Alice Walker; intro by Mary Helen Washington. Old Westbury, NY: Feminist, 1979.

Manuscripts & Archives

The major collections are at the Beinecke Library, Yale U; the U of Florida Library; & Howard U Library.

Biographies

BOOK

*Hemenway, Robert E. *ZNH: A Literary Biography.* Urbana: U Illinois P, 1977.

BOOK SECTIONS

Hughes, Langston. "Harlem Literati." *The Big Sea* (NY: Hill & Wang, 1940), 233–241. Excerpted Bloom (1986).

Neal, Larry. "Eatonville's ZNH: A Profile." *Black Review, No. 2* (NY: Morrow, 1972), 11–24.

ARTICLES

Burke, Virginia M. "ZNH and Fannie Hurst as They Saw Each Other." *College Language Association Journal,* 20 (Jun 1977), 435–447.

Helmick, Evelyn Thomas. "ZNH." *Carrell,* 11 (Jun–Dec 1970), 1–19.

Hurst, Fannie. "ZNH: A Personality Sketch." *Yale University Library Gazette,* 35 (Jul 1960), 17–22. Rpt Bloom (1986).

Pratt, Theodore. "ZNH." *Florida Historical Quarterly,* 40 (Jul 1961), 35–40. Rpt *Negro Digest,* 11 (Feb 1962), 52–56.

Southerland, Ellease. "The Novelist-Anthropologist's Life/Works: ZNH." *Black World,* 23 (Aug 1974), 20–30.

*Walker, Alice. "In Search of ZNH." *Ms,* 3 (Mar 1975), 74–79, 85–89. Rpt as "Looking for Zora," *I Love Myself When I Am Laughing . . .* Rpt Bloom (1986).

Wilentz, Gay. "White Patron and Black Artist: The Correspondence of Fannie Hurst and ZNH." *Library Chronicle of the University of Texas,* no 35 (1986), 20–43.

Critical Studies

BOOKS

*Holloway, Karla F C. *The Character of the Word: The Texts of ZNH.* NY: Greenwood, 1987.

*Howard, Lillie P. *ZNH.* Boston: Twayne, 1980.

COLLECTIONS OF ESSAYS

*Awkward, Michael, ed. *New Essays on Their Eyes Were Watching God.* Cambridge: Cambridge U P, 1990.

*Bloom, Harold, ed. *ZNH*. NY: Chelsea House, 1986.

Bloom. *ZNH's Their Eyes Were Watching God*. NY: Chelsea House, 1987.

Glassman, Steve & Kathryn Lee Seidel, eds. *Zora in Florida*. Orlando: U Central Florida, 1991.

SPECIAL JOURNAL

The Zora Neale Hurston Forum (annually, 1986–).

BOOK SECTIONS

*Awkward, Michael. "'The inaudible voice of it all': Silence, Voice, and Action in *Their Eyes Were Watching God*." *Studies in Black American Literature, Volume III: Black Feminist Criticism and Critical Theory*, ed Joe Weixlmann & Houston A Baker, Jr (Greenwood, Fla: Penkevill, 1988), 57–109.

Baum, Rosalie. "The Shape of H's Fiction." Glassman & Seidel, 94–109.

Bell, Bernard. "ZNH." *The Afro-American Novel and Its Tradition* (Amherst: U Massachusetts P, 1987), 119–128.

*Bethel, Lorraine. "'This Infinity of Conscious Pain': ZNH and the Black Female Literary Tradition." *But Some of Us Are Brave*, ed Gloria T Hull, Patricia Bell Scott & Barbara Smith (Old Westbury, NY: Feminist, 1982), 176–188. Rpt Bloom (1987).

*Boas, Franz. Preface. *Mules & Men*, x. Rpt Bloom (1986).

*Bone, Robert. "Aspects of the Racial Past." *The Negro Novel in America* (New Haven, Conn: Yale U P, 1958), 120–152. Rpt as "Ships at a Distance: The Meaning of *Their Eyes Were Watching God*," Bloom (1986).

*Brawley, Benjamin. *The Negro Genius* (NY: Biblo & Tannen, 1966), 257–259. Rpt as "One of the New Realists," Bloom (1986).

*Callahan, John F. "'Mah Tongue Is in Mah Friend's Mouff': The Rhetoric of Intimacy and Immensity in *Their Eyes Were Watching God*." Bloom (1987), 87–113.

Carson, Warren J. "H as Dramatist: The Florida Connection." Glassman & Siedel, 121–129.

*Cooke, Michael G. "The Beginnings of Self-Realization in ZNH, Richard Wright, and Ralph Ellison." *Afro–American Literature in the Twentieth Century* (New Haven, Conn: Yale U P, 1984), 71–109. Rpt as "The Beginnings of Self-Realization," Bloom (1986).

Duplessis, Rachel Blau. "Power, Judgment, and Narrative in a Work of ZNH: Feminist Cultural Studies." Awkward, 95–123.

Hemenway, Robert E. "ZNH and the Eatonville Anthropology." *The Harlem Renaissance Remembered*, ed Arna Bontemps (NY: Dodd, Mead, 1972), 190–214.

*Hemenway. "That Which the Soul Lives By." *Mules & Men* (Bloomington: Indiana U P, 1978), xi–xxviii. Rpt Bloom (1986).

Hemenway. "Are You a Flying Lark or a Setting Dove?" *Afro–American Literature*, ed Dexter Fisher & Robert B Stepto (NY: MLA, 1979), 122–152.

Hemenway. "The Personal Dimension in *Their Eyes Were Watching God*." Awkward, 29–49.

*Jackson, Blyden. Introduction. *Moses, Man of the Mountain* (Chicago: U Illinois P, 1984), vii–xix. Rpt Bloom (1986).

*Johnson, Barbara. "Metaphor, Metonymy, and Voice in *Their Eyes Were Watching God*." *Black Literature and Literary Theory*, ed Henry Louis Gates, Jr (NY: Methuen, 1984), 205–219. Rpt *Textual Analysis: Some Readers Reading*, ed Mary Ann Caws (NY: MLA, 1986). Rpt Bloom (1986), Bloom (1987).

*Johnson & Henry Louis Gates, Jr. "A Black and Idiomatic Free Indirect Discourse." Bloom (1987), 73–85.

Koenen, Anne & Sabine Bröck. "Alice Walker in Search of ZNH: Rediscovering a Black Female Literary Tradition." *History and Tradition in Afro-American Culture*, ed Günter H Lenz (Frankfurt, Germany: Campus Verlag, 1984), 167–180.

McKay, Nellie. "'Crayon Enlargements of Life': ZNH's *Their Eyes Were Watching God* as Autobiography." Awkward, 51–70.

*Meese, Elizabeth A. "Orality and Textuality in ZNH's *Their Eyes Were Watching God*." *Crossing the Double-Cross* (Chapel Hill: U North Carolina P, 1986), 41–53. Rpt Bloom (1987).

*Neal, Larry. Introduction. *Jonah's Gourd Vine* (NY: Lippincott, 1971), 5–7. Rpt as "The Spirituality of *Jonah's Gourd Vine*," Bloom (1986).

Pryse, Marjorie. "ZNH, Alice Walker, and the 'Ancient Power' of Black Women." *Conjuring: Black Women, Fiction and Literary Tradition*, ed Pryse & Hortense J Spillers (Bloomington: Indiana U P, 1985), 1–24.

Raynaud, Claudine. "Autobiography as 'Lying' Session: ZNH's *Dust Tracks on a Road*." *Studies in Black American Literature, Volume III: Black Feminist Criticism and Critical Theory*, ed Joe Weixlmann & Houston A Baker, Jr (Greenwood, Fla: Penkevill, 1988), 111–138.

*Rosenblatt, Roger. "*Their Eyes Were Watching God*." *Black Fiction* (Cambridge, Mass: Harvard U P, 1974), 84–90. Rpt Bloom (1986).

Seidel, Kathryn Lee. "The Artist in the Kitchen: The Economics of Creativity in H's 'Sweat.'" Glassman & Seidel, 110–120.

Southerland, Ellease. "The Influence of Voodoo on the Fiction of ZNH." *Sturdy Black Bridges,* ed Roseann P Bell, Bettye J Parker & Beverly Guy-Sheftall (Garden City, NY: Anchor/Doubleday, 1979), 171–183.

Turner, Darwin T. "ZNH, the Wandering Minstrel." *In a Minor Chord* (Carbondale: Southern Illinois U P, 1971), 89–120.

Wainwright, Mary Katherine. "Subversive Female Folk Tellers in *Mules & Men.*" Glassman & Seidel, 62–75.

*Walker, Alice. "ZNH—A Cautionary Tale and a Partisan View." Hemenway, *ZNH,* xi–xx. Rpt Bloom (1986).

*Walker. "On Refusing to Be Humbled by Second Place in a Contest You Did Not Design: A Tradition by Now." *I Love Myself When I Am Laughing . . . ,* 1–5. Rpt Bloom (1986).

Washington, Mary Helen. Introduction. *Black-Eyed Susans: Classic Stories By and About Black Women* (Garden City, NY: Doubleday, 1975), ix–xxxiii.

*Washington. "ZNH: A Woman Half in Shadow." *I Love Myself When I Am Laughing . . . ,* 7–25. Rpt Bloom (1986).

*Wilentz, Gay. "Defeating the False God: Janie's Self-Determination in ZNH's *Their Eyes Were Watching God.*" *Faith of a (Woman) Writer,* ed Alice Kessler-Harris & William McBrien (Westport, Conn: Greenwood, 1988), 285–291.

*Williams, Sherley Anne. "Foreword." *Their Eyes Were Watching God* (Chicago: U Illinois P, 1978), v–xv. Rpt Bloom (1986).

ARTICLES

Brown, Lloyd W. "ZNH and the Nature of Female Perception." *Obsidian,* 4 (Winter 1978), 39–45.

Crabtree, Claire. "The Confluence of Folklore, Feminism, and Black Self-Determination in ZNH's *Their Eyes Were Watching God.*" *Southern Literary Journal,* 17 (Spring 1985), 54–66.

Dandridge, Rita B. "Male Critics/Black Women's Novels." *College Language Association Journal,* 23 (Sep 1979), 1–11.

Ferguson, SallyAnn. "Folkloric Men and Female Growth in *Their Eyes Were Watching God.*" *Black American Literature Forum,* 21 (Spring–Summer 1987), 185–197.

Howard, Lillie P. "Marriage: ZNH's System of Values." *College Language Association Journal,* 21 (Dec 1977), 256–268.

Jackson, Blyden. "Some Negroes in the Land of Goshen." *Tennessee Folklore Society Bulletin,* 19 (Dec 1953), 103–107.

Jordan, Jennifer. "Feminist Fantasies: ZNH's *Their Eyes Were Watching God.*" *Tulsa Studies in Women's Literature,* 7 (Spring 1988), 105–117.

Kalb, John D. "The Anthropological Narrator of H's *Their Eyes Were Watching God.*" *Studies in American Fiction,* 16 (Autumn 1988), 169–180.

Kitch, Sally L. "Gender and Language: Dialect, Silence and the Disruption of Discourse." *Women's Studies,* 14, no 1 (1987), 65–78.

Krasner, James. "The Life of Women: ZNH and Female Autobiography." *Black American Literature Forum,* 23 (Spring 1989), 113–126.

*Kubitschek, Missy Dehn. "'Tuh de horizon and back': The Female Quest in *Their Eyes Were Watching God.*" *Black American Literature Forum,* 17 (Fall 1983), 109–115. Rpt Bloom (1987).

*Love, Theresa R. "ZNH's America." *Papers on Language and Literature,* 12 (Fall 1976), 422–437. Rpt Bloom (1986).

*Pondrom, Cyrena N. "The Role of Myth in H's *Their Eyes Were Watching God.*" *American Literature,* 58 (May 1986), 181–202.

Rayson, Ann. "*Dust Tracks on a Road:* ZNH and the Form of Black Autobiography." *Negro American Literature Forum,* 7 (Summer 1973), 39–45.

Smith, Barbara. "Sexual Politics and the Fiction of ZNH." *Radical Teacher,* 8 (May 1978), 26–30.

Stetson, Erlene. "*Their Eyes Were Watching God:* A Woman's Story." *Regionalism and the Female Imagination,* 4 (1978), 30–36.

Urgo, Joseph R. "'The Tune Is the Unity of the Thing': Power and Vulnerability in ZNH's *Their Eyes Were Watching God.*" *Southern Literary Journal,* 23 (Spring 1991), 40–54.

Wald, Priscilla. "Becoming 'Colored': The Self-Authorized Language of Difference in ZNH." *American Literary History,* 2 (Spring 1990), 79–100.

Walker, S Jay. "ZNH's *Their Eyes Were Watching God:* Black Novel of Sexism." *Modern Fiction Studies,* 20 (Winter 1974–1975), 519–527.

Wall, Cheryl A. "*Mules & Men* and Women: ZNH's Strategies of Narration and Visions of Female Empowerment." *Black American Literature Forum,* 23 (Winter 1989), 661–680.

*Washington, Mary Helen. "ZNH: The Black Woman's Search for Identity." *Black World,* 21 (Aug 1972), 68–75.

— *Ellen M. Millsaps*

TONI MORRISON

Lorain, Ohio, 18 Feb 1931–

Toni Morrison has achieved both popular success and critical acclaim for her work as a novelist. Her literary reputation rests on her ability to represent the complexity of African American life and culture by means of history, myth, and folklore. Morrison is known for her intricate plots, sensitively drawn characters, and lyrical prose echoing black vernacular language. Her fiction examines the racism and sexism of Western culture while exploring the ways in which ordinary black men and women resist oppression and reconcile the claims of the individual with those of the community. While early criticism focused primarily on Morrison's themes, more recent scholarship has examined her rhetorical strategies and the relationship between her novels and those of other writers in the black women's literary tradition. Morrison received the Nobel Prize for Literature in 1993.

Bibliography

*Middleton, David L. *TM: An Annotated Bibliography*. NY: Garland, 1987. Primary & secondary.

Books

The Bluest Eye. NY & c: Holt, Rinehart & Winston, 1970. Novel.

Sula. NY: Knopf, 1974. Novel.

Song of Solomon. NY: Knopf, 1977. Novel.

Tar Baby. NY: Knopf, 1981. Novel.

Beloved. NY: Knopf, 1987. Novel.

Jazz. NY: Knopf, 1992. Novel.

Playing in the Dark: Whiteness and the Literary Imagination. Cambridge, Mass & London: Harvard U P, 1992. Lectures.

Other

Race-ing Justice, En-gendering Power: Essays on Anita Hill, Clarence Thomas, and the Construction of Social Reality, ed with intro by TM. NY: Pantheon, 1992.

Interviews

BOOK SECTIONS

Koenen, Anne. "'The One Out of Sequence': An Interview With TM, New York, April 1980." *History and Tradition in Afro-American Culture,* ed Günter H Lenz (Frankfurt, Germany: Campus Verlag, 1984), 207–221.

McCluskey, Audrey T. "A Conversation With TM." *Women in the Arts* (Bloomington: Women's Studies Program, Indiana U, 1986), 82–88.

Parker, Bettye J. "Complexity: TM's Women—An Interview Essay." *Sturdy Black Bridges,* ed Roseann P Bell, Parker & Beverly Guy-Sheftall (Garden City, NY: Anchor/Doubleday, 1979), 251–257.

Ruas, Charles. "TM." *Conversations With American Writers* (NY: Knopf, 1985), 215–243.

Stepto, Robert B. "'Intimate Things in Place': A Conversation With TM." *Chant of Saints,* ed Michael S Harper & Stepto (Urbana: U Illinois P, 1979), 213–229.

Tate, Claudia. "TM." *Black Women Writers at Work* (NY: Continuum, 1983), 117–131.

ARTICLES

Bakerman, Jane. "The Seams Can't Show: An Interview With TM." *Black American Literature Forum,* 12 (Summer 1978), 56–60.

Darling, Marsha. "In the Realm of Responsibility: A Conversation With TM." *Women's Review of Books,* 5 (Mar 1988), 5–6.

Dowling, Colette. "The Song of TM." *New York Times Magazine* (20 May 1979), 40–42, 48, 52, 54, 56, 58.

LeClair, Thomas. "'The Language Must Not Sweat,'" *New Republic,* 184 (21 Mar 1981), 25–29.

McKay, Nellie. "An Interview With TM." *Contemporary Literature,* 24 (Winter 1983), 413–429.

Naylor, Gloria & TM. "A Conversation." *Southern Review,* 21 (Summer 1985), 567–593.

Watkins, Mel. "Talk With TM." *New York Times Book Review* (11 Sep 1977), 48, 50.

Wilson, Judith. "A Conversation With TM." *Essence,* 12 (Jul 1981), 84–86, 128, 130, 133–134.

Critical Studies

BOOKS

Butler-Evans, Elliott. *Race, Gender, and Desire: Narrative Strategies in the Fiction of Toni Cade Bambara, TM, and Alice Walker.* Philadelphia: Temple U P, 1989.

Holloway, Karla F C & Stephanie A Demetrakopoulos. *New Dimensions of Spirituality: A Biracial and Bicultural Reading of the Novels of TM.* NY: Greenwood, 1987.

Jones, Bessie W & Audrey L Vinson. *The World of TM: Explorations in Literary Criticism.* Dubuque, Iowa: Kendall/Hunt, 1985.

Mbalia, Doreatha D. *TM's Developing Class Consciousness.* Selinsgrove, Pa: Susquehanna U P / London: Associated U Presses, 1991.

*Mobley, Marilyn Sanders. *Folk Roots and Mythic Wings in Sarah Orne Jewett and TM: The Cultural Function of Narrative.* Baton Rouge: Louisiana State U P, 1991.

Otten, Terry. *The Crime of Innocence in the Fiction of TM.* Columbia: U Missouri P, 1989.

*Rigney, Barbara Hill. *The Voices of TM.* Columbus: Ohio State U P, 1991.

*Samuels, Wilfred D. *TM.* Boston: Twayne, 1990.

COLLECTIONS OF ESSAYS

*Bloom, Harold, ed. *TM.* NY: Chelsea House, 1990.

*McKay, Nellie, ed. *Critical Essays on TM.* Boston: Hall, 1988.

SPECIAL JOURNALS

Callaloo, 19 (Summer 1990), 471–525. TM Section.

Texas Studies in Literature and Language, 33 (Spring 1991), 89-123. TM Section.

BOOK SECTIONS

Awkward, Michael. "Roadblocks and Relatives: Critical Revision in TM's *The Bluest Eye.*" McKay, 57–68.

Barthold, Bonnie J. "TM, *Song of Solomon.*" *Black Time* (New Haven, Conn: Yale U P, 1981), 174–184.

Bell, Bernard. "Chloe Anthony 'Toni' M." *The Afro-American Novel and Its Tradition* (Amherst: U Massachusetts P, 1987), 270–277.

Byerman, Keith E. "Beyond Realism: The Fictions of Gayl Jones and TM." *Fingering the Jagged Grain* (Athens: U Georgia P, 1985), 171–216. Excerpted Bloom.

*Christian, Barbara. "The Contemporary Fables of TM." *Black Women Novelists* (Westport, Conn: Greenwood, 1980), 137–179.

Christian. "The Concept of Class in the Novels of TM." *Black Feminist Criticism* (NY: Pergamon, 1985), 71–80.

*Denard, Carolyn. "The Convergence of Feminism and Ethnicity in the Fiction of TM." McKay, 171–179.

Fabre, Genevieve. "Genealogical Archaeology or the Quest for Legacy in TM's *Song of Solomon.*" McKay, 105–114.

Grant, Robert. "Absence into Presence: The Thematics of Memory and 'Missing' Subjects in TM's *Sula.*" McKay, 90–103.

Harris, Trudier. "Reconnecting Fragments: Afro-American Folk Tradition in *The Bluest Eye.*" McKay, 68–76.

*Lee, Dorothy H. "The Quest for Self: Triumph and Failure in the Works of TM." *Black Women Writers (1950–1980),* ed Mari Evans (Garden City, NY: Anchor/Doubleday, 1984), 346–360.

*McDowell, Deborah E. "'The Self and the Other': Reading TM's *Sula* and the Black Female Text." McKay, 77–90. Rpt Bloom.

Miner, Madonne M. "Lady No Longer Sings the Blues: Rape, Madness and Silence in *The Bluest Eye.*" *Conjuring,* ed Marjorie Pryse & Hortense J Spillers (Bloomington: Indiana U P, 1985), 176–191. Rpt Bloom.

*Mobley, Marilyn Sanders. "A Different Remembering: Memory, History and Meaning in TM's *Beloved.*" Bloom, 189–199.

O'Shaughnessy, Kathleen. "'Life life life life': The Community as Chorus in *Song of Solomon.*" McKay, 125–133.

Pinsker, Sanford. "Magic Realism, Historical Truth, and the Quest for a Liberating Identity: Reflections on Alex Haley's *Roots* and TM's *Song of Solomon.*" *Studies in Black American Literature, Volume I: Black American Prose Theory,* ed Joe Weixlmann & Charles J Fontenot (Greenwood, Fla: Penkevill, 1984), 183–197.

Reckley, Ralph. "On Looking Into M's *Tar Baby.*" *Amid Visions and Revisions,* ed Burney J Hollis (Baltimore, Md: Morgan State U P, 1985), 132–138.

Skerrett, Joseph T, Jr. "Recitation to the Griot: Storytelling and Learning in TM's *Song of Solomon.*" *Conjuring,* ed Marjorie Pryse & Hortense J Spillers (Bloomington: Indiana U P, 1985), 192–202.

*Smith, Valerie. "TM's Narratives of Community." *Self-Discovery and Authority in Afro-American Narrative* (Cambridge, Mass: Harvard U P, 1987), 122–153, 163–164.

Traylor, Eleanor W. "The Fabulous World of TM: *Tar Baby.*" *Confirmation,* ed Amiri & Amina Baraka (NY: Quill, 1983), 333–352.

*Turner, Darwin T. "Theme, Characterization, and Style in the Works of TM." *Black Women Writers (1950–1980),* ed Mari Evans (Garden City, NY: Anchor/Doubleday, 1984), 316–369.

Wagner, Linda W. "TM: Mastery of Narrative." *Contemporary American Women Writers,* ed Catherine Rainwater & William J Scheick (Lexington: U P Kentucky, 1985), 191–207.

Werner, Craig. "The Briar Patch as Modernist Myth: M, Barthes and Tar Baby As-Is." McKay, 150–167.

*Wilkerson, Margaret B. "The Dramatic Voice in TM's Novels." McKay, 179–190.

ARTICLES

*Bakerman, Jane S. "Failures of Love: Female Initiation in the Novels of TM." *American Literature,* 52 (Jan 1981), 541–563.

Bischoff, Joan. "The Novels of TM: Studies in Thwarted Sensitivity." *Studies in Black Literature,* 6 (Fall 1975), 21–23.

Blake, Susan L. "Folklore and Community in *Song of Solomon.*" *MELUS,* 7 (Fall 1980), 77–82.

Brenner, Gerry. "*Song of Solomon:* M's Rejection of Rank's Monomyth and Feminism." *Studies in American Fiction,* 15 (Spring 1987), 13–24. Rpt McKay.

Bulsterbaum, Allison. "'Sugarman Gone Home': Folksong in TM's *Song of Solomon.*" *Publications of the Arkansas Philological Association,* 10 (Spring 1984), 15–28.

Butler, Robert James. "Open Movement and Selfhood in TM's *Song of Solomon.*" *Centennial Review,* 28–29 (Fall–Winter 1984–1985), 58–75.

Christian, Barbara. "Community and Nature: The Novels of TM." *Journal of Ethnic Studies,* 7 (Winter 1980), 65–78. Rpt *Black Feminist Criticism* by Christian (NY: Pergamon, 1985).

*Clark, Norris. "Flying Black: TM's *The Bluest Eye, Sula* and *Song of Solomon.*" *Minority Voices,* 4 (Fall 1980), 51–63.

Coleman, James. "The Quest for Wholeness in TM's *Tar Baby.*" *Black American Literature Forum,* 20 (Spring–Summer 1986), 63–73.

*Davis, Cynthia A. "Self, Society and Myth in TM's Fiction." *Contemporary Literature,* 23 (Summer 1982), 323–342. Rpt Bloom.

DeArman, Charles. "Milkman as the Archetypal Hero: 'Thursday's Child Has Far to Go.'" *Obsidian,* 6 (Winter 1980), 56–59.

DeWeever, Jacqueline. "The Inverted World of TM's *The Bluest Eye* and *Sula.*" *College Language Association Journal,* 22 (Jun 1979), 402–414.

DeWeever. "TM's Use of Fairy Tale, Folk Tale and Myth in *Song of Solomon.*" *Southern Folklore Quarterly,* 44 (1980), 131–144.

*Edelberg, Cynthia Dubin. "M's Voices: Formal Education, the Work Ethic, and the Bible." *American Literature,* 58 (May 1986), 217–237.

Erickson, Peter B. "Image of Nurturance in TM's *Tar Baby.*" *College Language Association Journal,* 28 (Sep 1984), 11–32.

Harris, A Leslie. "Myth as Structure in TM's *Song of Solomon.*" *MELUS,* 7 (Fall 1980), 69–76.

Hawthorne, Evelyn. "On Gaining the Double-Vision: *Tar Baby* as Diasporean Novel." *Black American Literature Forum,* 22 (Spring 1988), 97–107.

*House, Elizabeth B. "The 'Sweet Life' in TM's Fiction." *American Literature,* 56 (May 1984), 181–202.

Hovet, Grace Ann & Barbara Lounsberry. "Flying as Symbol and Legend in TM's *The Bluest Eye, Sula,* and *Song of Solomon.*" *College Language Association Journal,* 27 (Dec 1983), 119–140.

*Iannone, Carol. "TM's Career." *Commentary,* 84 (Dec 1987), 59–63.

Joyce, Joyce Ann. "Structural and Thematic Unity in TM's *Song of Solomon.*" *CEA Critic,* 49 (Winter–Summer 1986–1987), 185–198.

Lange, Bonnie Shipman. "TM's Rainbow Code." *Critique,* 24 (Spring 1983), 173–181.

Lee, Dorothy H. "*Song of Solomon:* To Ride the Air." *Black American Literature Forum,* 16 (1982), 64–70.

Lepow, Lauren. "Paradise Lost and Found: Dualism and Edenic Myth in TM's *Tar Baby.*" *Contemporary Literature,* 28 (Fall 1987), 363–377.

Levy, Andrew. "Telling *Beloved.*" *Texas Studies in Literature and Language,* 33 (Spring 1991), 114–123.

Lounsberry, Barbara & Grace Ann Hovet. "Principles of Perception in TM's *Sula*." *Black American Literature Forum,* 13 (Winter 1979), 126–129.

MacKethan, Lucinda H. "Names to Bear Witness: The Theme and Tradition of Naming in TM's *Song of Solomon*." *CEA Critic,* 49 (Winter–Summer 1986–1987), 199–207.

Marshall, Brenda. "The Gospel According to Pilate." *American Literature,* 57 (Oct 1985), 486–489.

Martin, Odette C. "*Sula*." *First World* (Winter 1977), 35–44.

Middleton, Victoria. "*Sula*: An Experimental Life." *College Language Association Journal,* 28 (Jun 1985), 367–381.

Mobley, Marilyn. "Narrative Dilemma: Jadine as Cultural Orphan in TM's *Tar Baby*." *Southern Review,* 23 (Autumn 1987), 761–770.

Munro, C Lynn. "The Tatooed Heart and the Serpentine Eye: M's Choice of an Epigraph for *Sula*." *Black American Literature Forum,* 18 (Winter 1984), 150–154.

Ogunyemi, Chikwenye Okonjo. "Order and Disorder in TM's *The Bluest Eye*." *Critique,* 19, no 1 (1977), 112–120.

O'Meally, Robert G. "'Tar Baby, She Don' Say Nothin'.'" *Callaloo,* 4 (Feb–Oct 1981), 193–198.

Portales, Marco. "TM's *The Bluest Eye*: Shirley Temple and Cholly." *Centennial Review,* 30 (Fall 1986), 496–506.

Rainwater, Catherine. "Worthy Messengers: Narrative Voices in TM's Novels." *Texas Studies in Literature and Language,* 33 (Spring 1991), 96–113.

Reyes, Angelita. "Ancient Properties in the New World: The Paradox of the 'Other' in TM's *Tar Baby*." *Black Scholar,* 17 (Mar–Apr 1986), 19–25.

Rosenberg, Ruth. "'And the Children May Know Their Names': TM's *Song of Solomon*." *Literary Onomastic Studies,* 8 (1981), 195–219.

Rosenberg. "Seeds in Hard Ground: Black Girlhood in *The Bluest Eye*." *Black American Literature Forum,* 21 (Winter 1987), 435–445.

Samuels, Wilfrid D. "Liminality and the Search for Self in TM's *Song of Solomon*." *Minority Voices,* 5 (Spring–Fall 1981), 59–68.

Scruggs, Charles. "The Nature of Desire in TM's *Song of Solomon*." *Arizona Quarterly,* 38 (Winter 1982), 311–335.

Shannon, Anna. "'We Was Girls Together': A Study of TM's *Sula*." *Midwestern Miscellany,* 10 (1982), 9–22.

Smith, Valerie. "The Quest for and Discovery of Identity in TM's *Song of Solomon*." *Southern Review,* 21 (Summer 1985), 721–732.

Stein, Karen. "TM's *Sula*: A Black Woman's Epic." *Black American Literature Forum,* 18 (Winter 1984), 146–150.

Strouse, Jean. "TM's Black Magic." *Newsweek,* 97 (30 Mar 1981), 52–57.

Willis, Susan. "Eruptions of Funk: Historicizing TM." *Black American Literature Forum,* 16 (Spring 1982), 34–42. Rpt *Black Literature and Literary Theory,* ed Henry Louis Gates, Jr (NY: Methuen, 1984). Augmented *Specifying* by Willis (Madison: U Wisconsin P, 1987).

— Marilyn Sanders Mobley
This entry has been revised and updated by the series editors.

ISHMAEL REED
Chattanooga, Tenn, 22 Feb 1938–

Ishmael Reed, a National Book Award nominee in both fiction and poetry, is recognized as one of America's major satirists. Using such devices as Egyptian symbols, Voodoo emanations, and Hoodoo icons, Reed attempts to explore the mythology of the African American's non-Western past in relation to American social and cultural traditions in general. Reed's fiction is noted for its inventive plots and language and for its often hilarious parodies.

Bibliography

*Settle, Elizabeth A & Thomas A. *IR: A Primary and Secondary Bibliography*. Boston: Hall, 1982.

Books

The Free-Lance Pallbearers. Garden City, NY: Doubleday, 1967. Novel.

Yellow Back Radio Broke-Down. Garden City, NY: Doubleday, 1969. Novel.

catechism of d neoamerican hoodoo church. London: Breman, 1970; Detroit, Mich: Broadside, 1971. Poems.

Conjure: Selected Poems, 1963–1970. Amherst: U Massachusetts P, 1972.

Mumbo Jumbo. Garden City, NY: Doubleday, 1972. Novel.

Chattanooga: Poems. NY: Random House, 1973.

The Last Days of Louisiana Red. NY: Random House, 1974. Novel.

Flight to Canada. NY: Random House, 1976. Novel.

A Secretary to the Spirits. NY & c: NOK, 1978. Poems.

Shrovetide in Old New Orleans. Garden City, NY: Doubleday, 1978. Essays.

God Made Alaska for the Indians. NY & London: Garland, 1982. Essays.

The Terrible Twos. NY: St Martin/Marek, 1982. Novel.

Mother Hubbard. NY: St Martin, 1982. Play.

The Ace Boons. NY: St Martin, 1983. Play.

Reckless Eyeballing. NY: St Martin, 1986. Novel.

Cab Calloway Stands In for the Moon. Flint, Mich: Bamberger, 1986. Poem.

Savage Wilds. NY: St Martin, 1986. Play.

Writin' Is Fightin'. NY: Atheneum, 1988. Essays.

New and Collected Poems. NY: Atheneum, 1988.

The Terrible Threes. NY: Atheneum, 1989. Novel.

Japanese by Spring. NY: Atheneum, 1993. Novel.

Other

The Rise, Fall, and . . . ? of Adam Clayton Powell, ed as by Emmett Coleman. NY: Bee-Line, 1967. Essays.

19 Necromancers From Now, ed with intro by IR. Garden City, NY: Doubleday, 1970. Anthology.

Yardbird Reader, Vols 1–5, ed IR. Berkeley, Calif: Y-Bird, 1971–1977. Anthologies.

Yardbird Lives! ed IR & Al Young. NY: Grove, 1978. Anthology.

Calafia: The California Poetry, ed IR. Berkeley, Calif: Y-Bird, 1979. Anthology.

Quilt, 5 vols, ed IR & Al Young. Berkeley, Calif: Quilt, 1981–1987. Anthologies.

The Before Columbus Foundation Fiction Anthology: Selections From the American Book Awards, 1980–1990, ed IR, Kathryn Trueblood & Shawn Wong. NY & London: Norton, 1992.

The Before Columbus Foundation Poetry Anthology: Selections From the American Book Awards, 1980–1990, ed J J Phillips, IR, Gundars Strads & Wong. NY & London: Norton, 1992.

Interviews

BOOK SECTIONS

*Bellamy, Joe David. "IR." *The New Fiction: Interviews With Innovative American Writers* (Urbana: U Illinois P, 1974), 130–141.

*Northouse, Cameron. "IR." *Conversations With Writers II* (Detroit, Mich: Bruccoli Clark/Gale, 1978), 212–254.

ARTICLES

*Bezner, Kevin. "An Interview With IR." *Mississippi Review,* 20, nos 1–2 (1991), 110–119.

Gover, Robert. "An Interview With IR." *Black American Literature Forum,* 12 (Spring 1978), 12–19.

"IR: A Conversation With John Domini." *American Poetry Review,* 7 (Jan–Feb 1978), 32–36.

Martin, Reginald. "An Interview With IR, Part I." *Review of Contemporary Fiction,* 4, no 2 (1984), 176–187.

Martin. "An Interview With IR, Part II." *Griot,* 7 (Spring 1988), 33–44.

*O'Brien, John. "IR: An Interview." *fiction international,* 1 (Fall 1973), 60–70. Rpt *Interviews With Black Writers* by O'Brien (NY: Liveright, 1973).

*"The Writer as Seer: IR on IR." *Black World,* 23 (Jun 1974), 20–34.

Critical Studies

BOOK

*Martin, Reginald. *IR and the New Black Aesthetic Critics.* NY: St Martin, 1988.

SPECIAL JOURNAL

Review of Contemporary Fiction, 4 (Summer 1984). IR/Juan Goytisolo issue.

BOOK SECTIONS

*Bell, Bernard W. "IR." *The Afro-American Novel and Its Tradition* (Amherst: U Massachusetts P, 1987), 329–336.

Cooke, Michael G. "Tragic and Ironic Denials of Intimacy: Jean Toomer, James Baldwin, and IR." *Afro-American Literature in the Twentieth Century* (New Haven, Conn: Yale U P, 1984), 177–199.

Gates, Henry Louis, Jr. "The Blackness of Black: A Critique on the Sign and the Signifying Monkey." *Figures in Black* (NY: Oxford U P, 1987), 235–276, 291–296.

*Klinkowitz, Jerome. "IR's Multicultural Aesthetic." *Literary Subversions* (Urbana: Southern Illinois U P, 1985), 18–33.

ARTICLES

Baraka, Amiri. "Afro-American Literature and Class Struggle." *Black American Literature Forum,* 14 (Spring 1980), 5–14.

Bravard, Robert S. "*Conjure: Selected Poems, 1963–1970.*" *Library Journal,* 97 (15 Dec 1972), 3992, 3994.

*Bryant, Jerry H. "Who? Jes Grew? Like Topsy? No, Not Like Topsy." *Nation,* 215 (25 Sep 1972), 245–247.

Cooper, Arthur. "Call Him Ishmael." *Newsweek,* 85 (2 Jun 1975), 70.

Dillingham, Thomas. "IR: *Chattanooga.*" *Open Places,* 16 (Winter 1973), 58–60.

Fabre, Michel. "IR's *Free-Lance Pallbearers* or the Dialectics of Shit." *Obsidian,* 3 (Winter 1977), 5–18.

Ford, Nick Aaron. "A Note on IR: Revolutionary Novelist." *Studies in the Novel,* 3 (Summer 1971), 216–218.

Harris, Norman. "The Gods Must Be Angry: *Flight to Canada* as Political History." *Modern Fiction Studies,* 34 (Spring 1988), 111–123.

Howe, Irving. "New Black Writers." *Harper's,* 29 (Dec 1969), 130–131, 133, 135, 137, 141, 144, 146.

Joye, Barbara. "Literature of Race and Culture: Satire and Alienation in Soulville." *Phylon,* 29, no 4 (1968), 410–412.

Mason, Theodore O, Jr. "Performance, History, and Myth: The Problem of IR's *Mumbo Jumbo.*" *Modern Fiction Studies,* 34 (Spring 1988), 97–109.

Reilly, John M. "The Reconstruction of Genre as Entry into Conscious History." *Black American Literature Forum,* 13 (Spring 1979), 3–6.

— Reginald Martin & Margaret Donovan DuPriest
This entry has been revised and updated by the series editors.

JEAN TOOMER
Washington, DC, 26 Dec 1894–Doylestown, Pa, 30 Mar 1967

Jean Toomer's reputation rests upon his first book, *Cane*, a mixture of prose and poetry published in 1923. *Cane*, which depicts African American rural and urban life, has been described as one of the most important works of the Harlem Renaissance and as a classic of American writing. While some early reviewers were puzzled by the book's stylistic innovations, most were impressed by its power and beauty. After 1923, Toomer, under the influence of esoteric thinker G. I. Gurdjieff, abandoned ethnic writing in favor of philosophical fiction and poetry dealing with spiritual themes and personal development. Toomer gained renewed critical attention with the republication of *Cane* in the 1960s and the discovery of previously unpublished material.

Bibliographies

Munro, C Lynn. "JT: A Bibliography of Secondary Sources." *Black American Literature Forum*, 21 (Fall 1987), 275–287.

Perry, Margaret. *The Harlem Renaissance: An Annotated Bibliography and Commentary* (NY: Garland, 1982), 138–158. Primary & secondary.

Reilly, John M. "JT: An Annotated Checklist of Criticism." *Resources for American Literary Study*, 4 (Spring 1974), 27–56.

Books

Cane. NY: Boni & Liveright, 1923. Miscellany.

Essentials: Definitions and Aphorisms. Chicago: Lakeside, 1931. Repub, ed Rudolph P Byrd. Athens & London: U Georgia P, 1991. Nonfiction.

An Interpretation of Friends Worship. Philadelphia: Committee on Religious Education of Friends General Conference, 1947. Essay.

The Flavor of Man. Philadelphia: Young Friends Movement of the Philadelphia Yearly Meetings, 1949. Lecture.

The Wayward and the Seeking: A Collection of Writings, ed with intro by Darwin T Turner. Washington: Howard U P, 1980. Miscellany.

The Collected Poems of JT, ed Robert B Jones & Margery Toomer Latimer; intro by Jones. Chapel Hill & London: U North Carolina P, 1988.

A JT Reader: Selected Unpublished Writings, ed with intro by Frederik L Rusch. NY & Oxford: Oxford U P, 1993.

Edition

*Cane: An Authoritative Text, Backgrounds, Criticism, ed Darwin T Turner. NY & London: Norton, 1988.

Manuscripts & Archives

Beinecke Library, Yale U.

Biographies

BOOKS

*Kerman, Cynthia Earl & Richard Eldridge. *The Lives of JT*. Baton Rouge: Louisiana State U P, 1987.

Larson, Charles R. *Invisible Darkness: JT and Nella Larsen*. Iowa City: U Iowa P, 1933.

BOOK SECTION

*Lewis, David Levering. "Stars." *When Harlem Was in Vogue* (NY: Knopf, 1981), 50–88.

Critical Studies

BOOKS

Benson, Brian Joseph & Mabel Mayle Dillard. *JT*. Boston: Twayne, 1980.

Byrd, Rudolph P. *JT's Years With Gurdjieff: Portrait of an Artist, 1923–1936.* Athens: U Georgia P, 1990.

Jones, Robert B. *JT and the Prison-House of Thought: A Phenomenology of the Spirit,* Amherst: U Massachusetts P, 1993.

*McKay, Nellie Y. *JT, Artist: A Study of His Life and Work, 1894–1936.* Chapel Hill: U North Carolina P, 1984.

COLLECTIONS OF ESSAYS

Durham, Frank, ed. *The Merrill Studies in Cane.* Columbus, Ohio: Merrill, 1971.

*O'Daniel, Therman B, ed. *JT: A Critical Evaluation.* Washington: Howard U P, 1988.

SPECIAL JOURNAL

College Language Association Journal, 17 (Jun 1974). JT issue.

BOOK SECTIONS

Baker, Houston. "Journey Toward Black Art: JT's *Cane.*" *Singers of Daybreak* (Washington: Howard U P, 1974), 53–80, 107–108.

Bone, Robert. "JT." *The Negro Novel in America* (New Haven, Conn: Yale U P, 1965), 80–89. Excerpted *Cane: An Authoritative Text, Backgrounds, Criticism.*

Bone. "JT." *Down Home* (NY: Putnam, 1975), 204–238, 301–303.

*Bontemps, Arna. "The Negro Renaissance: JT and the Harlem Writers of the 1920's." *Anger and Beyond,* ed Herbert Hill (NY: Harper & Row, 1966), 20–36. Rpt Durham. Excerpted *Cane: An Authoritative Text, Backgrounds, Criticism.*

Bowen, Barbara E. "Untroubled Voice: Call and Response in *Cane.*" *Black Literature and Literary Theory,* ed Henry Louis Gates, Jr (NY: Methuen, 1984), 187–203.

Cooke, Michael G. "Tragic and Ironic Denials of Intimacy: JT, James Baldwin, and Ishmael Reed." *Afro-American Literature in the Twentieth Century* (New Haven, Conn: Yale U P, 1984), 177–199.

Fullinwider, S P. "The Renaissance in Literature." *The Mind and Mood of Black America* (Homewood, Ill: Dorsey / Georgetown, Ontario: Irwin-Dorsey, 1969), 123–171.

Gibson, Donald B. "JT: The Politics of Denial." *The Politics of Literary Expression* (Westport, Conn: Greenwood, 1981), 155–181.

Gysin, Fritz. *The Grotesque in American Negro Fiction* (Bern, Switzerland: Franke, 1975), 36–90, 276–279, 288–296, 327.

Rosenfeld, Paul. "JT." *Men Seen* (NY: MacVeagh/Dial, 1925), 227–233. Rpt Durham.

Thompson, Larry E. "JT: As Modern Man." *The Harlem Renaissance Remembered*, ed Arna Bontemps (NY: Dodd, Mead, 1972), 51–62, 279.

*Turner, Darwin T. "JT: Exile." *In a Minor Chord* (Carbondale: Southern Illinois U P, 1971), 1–59, 121–132, 140–143. Excerpted *Cane: An Authoritative Text, Backgrounds, Criticism.*

Wagner, Jean. "JT." *Black Poets of the United States From Paul Laurence Dunbar to Langston Hughes,* trans Kenneth Douglas (Urbana: U Illinois P, 1973), 259–281, 531–532, 541–542.

ARTICLES

Ackley, Donald G. "Theme and Vision in JT's *Cane*." *Studies in Black Literature,* 1 (Spring 1970), 45–65.

Brinkmeyer, Robert H, Jr. "Wasted Talent, Wasted Art: The Literary Career of JT." *Southern Quarterly,* 20 (Fall 1981), 75–84.

Christensen, Peter. "Sexuality and Liberation in JT's 'Withered Skin of Berries.'" *Callaloo,* 11 (Summer 1988), 616–626.

Davis, Charles T. "JT and the South: Region and Race as Elements Within a Literary Imagination." *Studies in the Literary Imagination,* 17 (Fall 1974), 23–37.

Fullinwider, S P. "JT: Lost Generation, or Negro Renaissance?" *Phylon,* 27 (Winter 1966), 396–403. Rpt Durham, O'Daniel.

Golding, Alan. "JT's *Cane:* The Search for Identity Through Form." *Arizona Quarterly,* 39 (Autumn 1983), 197–214.

Morrison, Toni. "JT's Art of Darkness." *Washington Post Book World* (13 Jul 1980), 1, 13.

Reilly, John M. "The Search for Black Redemption: JT's *Cane*." *Studies in the Novel,* 2 (Fall 1970), 312–324. Rpt *Cane: An Authoritative Text, Backgrounds, Criticism.*

Rusch, Frederik L. "The Blue Man: JT's Solution to His Problems of Identity." *Obsidian,* 6 (Spring–Summer 1980), 38–54.

Rusch. "A Tale of the Country Round: JT's Legend, 'Monrovia.'" *MELUS,* 7 (Summer 1980), 37–46.

Rusch. "JT's Early Identification: The Two Black Plays." *MELUS*, 13 (Spring–Summer 1986), 115–124.

Scruggs, Charles W. "The Mark of Cain and the Redemption of Art: A Study in Theme and Structure of JT's *Cane*." *American Literature*, 44 (May 1972), 276–291.

Scruggs. "JT: Fugitive." *American Literature*, 47 (Mar 1975), 84–96.

Taylor, Clyde. "The Second Coming of JT." *Obsidian*, 1 (Winter 1975), 37–57.

Turner, Darwin T. "The Failure of a Playwright." *College Language Association Journal*, 10 (Jun 1967), 308–318. Rpt Durham, O'Daniel.

— *Frederik L. Rusch*

ALICE WALKER
Eatonton, Ga, 9 Feb 1944–

Alice Walker occupies a central position in the emergence of African American women's writing during the 1970s and 1980s. Best known as a novelist, Walker has also received serious attention as a poet, short-story writer, and essayist. Popular both with academic critics and the general reading public, Walker's epistolary novel *The Color Purple* established her as a leading figure in what she labeled a "womanist" movement. In part because she had attracted a substantial audience through her work with *Ms.* magazine, the essays collected in Walker's *In Search of Our Mothers' Gardens,* especially her celebration of Zora Neale Hurston, have assumed a central role in recent discussions of the relationship between issues of race and gender.

Bibliographies

Banks, Erma Davis & Keith Byerman. *AW: An Annotated Bibliography.* NY: Garland, 1989. Primary & secondary.

Kirschner, Susan. "AW's Nonfictional Prose: A Checklist, 1966–1984." *Black American Literature Forum,* 18 (Winter 1984), 162–163. Primary.

Pratt, Louis H & Darrell D. *Alice Malsenior Walker: An Annotated Bibliography, 1968–1986.* Westport, Conn: Meckler, 1988. Primary & secondary.

Books

Once: Poems. NY: Harcourt, Brace & World, 1968.

The Third Life of Grange Copeland. NY: Harcourt Brace Jovanovich, 1970. Novel.

In Love and Trouble: Stories of Black Women. NY: Harcourt Brace Jovanovich, 1973.

Revolutionary Petunias and Other Poems. NY: Harcourt Brace Jovanovich, 1973.

Langston Hughes, American Poet. NY: Crowell, 1974. Children's biography.

Meridian. NY & London: Harcourt Brace Jovanovich, 1976. Novel.

Good Night, Willie Lee, I'll See You in the Morning. NY: Dial, 1979. Poetry.

You Can't Keep a Good Woman Down. NY & London: Harcourt Brace Jovanovich, 1981. Stories.

The Color Purple. NY & London: Harcourt Brace Jovanovich, 1982. Novel.

In Search of Our Mothers' Gardens: Womanist Prose. San Diego & c: Harcourt Brace Jovanovich, 1983.

Horses Make a Landscape Look More Beautiful: Poems. San Diego & c: Harcourt Brace Jovanovich, 1984.

Living by the Word: Selected Writings, 1973–1987. San Diego & c: Harcourt Brace Jovanovich, 1988.

The Temple of My Familiar. San Diego & c: Harcourt Brace Jovanovich, 1989. Novel.

Her Blue Body Everything We Know: Earthling Poems, 1965–1990, Complete. San Diego & c: Harcourt Brace Jovanovich, 1991.

Possessing the Secret of Joy. New York & c: Harcourt Brace Jovanovich, 1992. Novel.

Other

I Love Myself When I Am Laughing . . . and Then Again When I Am Looking Mean and Impressive: A Zora Neale Hurston Reader, ed AW. Old Westbury, NY: Feminist, 1979.

Biography

ARTICLE

Steinem, Gloria. "Do You Know This Woman? She Knows You: A Profile of AW." *Ms.,* 10 (Jun 1982), 35, 37, 89–94.

Critical Studies

BOOKS

Butler-Evans, Elliott. *Race, Gender, and Desire: Narrative Strategies in the Fiction of Toni Cade Bambara, Toni Morrison, and AW*. Philadelphia: Temple U P, 1989.

*Winchell, Donna. *AW*. NY: Twayne, 1992.

COLLECTIONS OF ESSAYS

*Bloom, Harold, ed. *AW*. NY: Chelsea House, 1989.

*Gates, Henry Louis, Jr & K A Appiah, eds. *AW: Critical Perspectives Past and Present*. NY: Amistad, 1993.

BOOK SECTIONS

*Awkward, Michael. "*The Color Purple* and the Achievement of (Comm)unity." *Inspiriting Influences: Tradition, Revision, and Afro-American Women's Novels* (NY: Columbia U P, 1989), 135–164.

*Byerman, Keith E. "Women's Blues: The Fiction of Toni Cade Bambara and AW." *Fingering the Jagged Grain: Tradition and Form in Recent Black Fiction* (Athens: U Georgia P, 1985), 128–170.

Byrd, Rudolph P. "Spirituality in the Novels of AW: Models, Healing and Transformation, or When the Spirit Moves So Do We." *Wild Women in the Whirlwind: Afra-American Culture and the Contemporary Literary Renaissance,* ed Joanne M Braxton & Andree Nicola McLaughlin (New Brunswick, NJ: Rutgers U P, 1990), 363–378.

*Callahan, John F. "The Hoop of Language: Politics and the Restoration of Voice in *Meridian*." *In the African-American Grain: The Pursuit of Voice in Twentieth-Century Black Fiction* (Urbana: U Illinois P, 1988), 217–255.

*Christian, Barbara. "Novels for Everyday Use: The Novels of AW." *Black Women Novelists: The Development of a Tradition, 1892–1976* (Westport, Conn: Greenwood, 1980), 180–238. Rpt Gates & Appiah.

*Christian. "AW: The Black Woman Artist as Wayward." *Black Women Writers (1950–1980),* ed Mari Evans (Garden City, NY: Anchor/Doubleday, 1984), 457–477. Rpt Bloom.

Christian. "The Contrary Women of AW: A Study of Female Protagonists in *In Love and Trouble*." *Black Feminist Criticism* (NY: Pergamon, 1985), 31–46.

Collins, Gina Michelle. "*The Color Purple:* What Feminism Can Learn From a Southern Tradition." *Southern Literature and Literary Theory,* ed Jefferson Humphries (Athens: U Georgia P, 1990), 75–87.

Cooke, Michael G. "Intimacy: The Interpenetration of the One and the All in Robert Hayden and AW." *Afro-American Literature in the Twentieth Century: The Achievement of Intimacy* (New Haven, Conn: Yale U P, 1984), 133–176.

Dixon, Melvin. "Keep Me From Sinking Down: Zora Neale Hurston, AW, and Gayl Jones." *Ride Out the Wilderness: Geography and Identity in Afro-American Literature* (Urbana: U Illinois P, 1987), 83–120.

*DuPlessis, Rachel Blau. "Beyond the Hard Visible Horizon." *Writing Beyond the Ending: Narrative Strategies of Twentieth-Century Women Writers* (Bloomington: Indiana U P, 1985), 142–161.

Fifer, Elizabeth. "The Dialect and Letters of *The Color Purple*." *Contemporary American Women Writers: Narrative Strategies,* ed Catherine Rainwater & William J Scheick (Lexington: U P Kentucky, 1985), 155–171.

*Gates, Henry Louis, Jr. "Color Me Zora: AW's (Re) Writing of the Speakerly Text." *The Signifying Monkey: A Theory of Afro-American Literary Criticism* (NY: Oxford U P, 1988), 239–258. Rpt Gates & Appiah.

Harris, Norman. "Three Black Women Writers and Humanism: A Folk Perspective." *Black American Literature and Humanism,* ed R Baxter Miller (Lexington: U P Kentucky, 1981), 50–74.

Harris. "*Meridian:* Answers in the Black Church." *Connecting Times: The Sixties in Afro-American Fiction* (Jackson: U P Mississippi, 1988), 98–119.

Hernton, Calvin C. "Who's Afraid of AW? *The Color Purple* as Slave Narrative." *The Sexual Mountain and Black Women Writers* (Garden City, NY: Anchor/Doubleday, 1987), 1–36.

*Hite, Molly. "Romance, Marginality, and Matrilineage: AW's *The Color Purple* and Zora Neale Hurston's *Their Eyes Were Watching God*." *Reading Black, Reading Feminist,* ed Henry Louis Gates, Jr (NY: Meridian, 1990), 431–453.

*Hooks, Bell. "Writing the Subject: Reading *The Color Purple*." *Reading Black, Reading Feminist,* ed Henry Louis Gates, Jr (NY: Meridian, 1990), 454–470. Rpt Gates & Appiah.

Jones, Gayl. "Blues and Spirituals: Dramatic and Lyrical Patterns in AW's *The Third Life of Grange Copeland.*" *Liberating Voices: Oral Tradition in African American Literature* (Cambridge, Mass: Harvard U P, 1991), 151–160.

*Kubitschek, Missy Dehn. "Every Mother a Daughter." *Claiming the Heritage: African-American Women Novelists and History* (Jackson: U P Mississippi, 1991), 143–177.

McKay, Nellie. "AW's 'Advancing Luna—and Ida B. Wells': A Struggle Toward Sisterhood." *Rape and Representation,* ed Lynn A Higgins & Brenda R Silver (NY: Columbia U P, 1991), 248–260.

O'Brien, John. "AW." *Interviews With Black Writers* (NY: Liveright, 1973), 185–211. Rpt Gates & Appiah.

Parker-Smith, Bettye J. "AW's Women: In Search of Some Peace of Mind." *Black Women Writers (1950–1980),* ed Mari Evans (Garden City, NY: Anchor/Doubleday, 1984), 478–493.

Spillers, Hortense J. "'The Permanent Obliquity of an In(pha)llibly Straight': In the Time of the Daughters and the Fathers." *Changing Our Own Words: Essays on Criticism, Theory, and Writing by Black Women,* ed Cheryl A Wall (New Brunswick, NJ: Rutgers U P, 1989), 127–149.

Tate, Claudia. "AW." *Black Women Writers at Work,* ed Tate (NY: Continuum, 1983), 175–187.

Wade-Gayles, Gloria Jean. *No Crystal Stair: Visions of Race and Sex in Black Women's Fiction* (NY: Pilgrim, 1984), 102–113, 199–215.

Walker, Melissa. *Down From the Mountaintop: Black Women's Novels in the Wake of the Civil Rights Movement, 1966–1989* (New Haven, Conn: Yale U P, 1991), 60–73, 167–180.

Wallace, Michele. "Blues for Mr. Spielberg." *Invisibility Blues* (NY: Verso, 1990), 67–76.

*Washington, Mary Helen. "An Essay on AW." *Sturdy Black Bridges,* ed Roseann P Bell, Bettye J Parker & Beverly Guy-Sheftall (Garden City, NY: Anchor/Doubleday, 1979), 133–156. Rpt Gates & Appiah.

Washington. "I Sign My Mother's Name: AW, Dorothy West, Paule Marshall." *Mothering the Mind: Twelve Studies of Writers and Their Silent Partners,* ed Ruth Perry & Martine Watson Brownley (NY: Holmes & Meier, 1984), 142–163.

Wilentz, Gay. "AW: *The Color Purple.*" *Binding Cultures: Black Women Writers in Africa and the Diaspora* (Bloomington: Indiana U P, 1992), 61–80.

Willis, Susan. "AW's Women." *Specifying: Black Women Writing the American Experience* (Madison: U Wisconsin P, 1987), 110–128.

ARTICLES

Berlant, Lauren. "Race, Gender, and Nation in *The Color Purple.*" *Critical Inquiry,* 14 (Summer 1988), 831–859. Rpt Gates & Appiah.

Bobo, Jacqueline. "Sifting Through the Controversy: Reading *The Color Purple.*" *Callaloo,* 12 (Spring 1989), 332–342.

*Bradley, David. "Novelist AW Telling the Black Woman's Story." *New York Times Magazine* (8 Jan 1984), 24–36.

Butler, Robert James. "Making a Way Out of No Way: The Journey in AW's *The Third Life of Grange Copeland.*" *Black American Literature Forum,* 22 (Spring 1988), 65–79.

Byerman, Keith E. "Desire and AW: The Quest for a Womanist Narrative." *Callaloo,* 12 (Spring 1989), 321–331.

Chambers, Kimberly. "Right on Time: History and Religion in AW's *The Color Purple.*" *College Language Association Journal,* 31 (Sep 1987), 44–62.

Danielson, Susan. "AW's *Meridian,* Feminism, and the 'Movement.'" *Women's Studies,* 16 (Oct 1989), 317–330.

*Davis, Thadious M. "AW's Celebration of Self in Southern Generations." *Southern Quarterly,* 21 (Summer 1983), 39–53. Rpt Bloom.

*Erickson, Peter. "'Cast Out Alone/ To Heal/ And Re-Create/ Ourselves': Family-Based Identity in the Work of AW." *College Language Association Journal,* 23 (Sep 1979), 71–94. Rpt Bloom.

*Froula, Christine. "The Daughter's Seduction: Sexual Violence and Literary History." *Signs,* 11 (Summer 1986), 621–644.

Gaston, Karen C. "Women in the Lives of Grange Copeland." *College Language Association Journal,* 24 (Mar 1981), 276–286.

Hamilton, Cynthia. "AW's Politics or the Politics of *The Color Purple.*" *Journal of Black Studies,* 18 (Mar 1988), 379–391.

Harris, Trudier. "Folklore in the Fiction of AW: A Perpetuation of Historical and Literary Traditions." *Black American Literature Forum,* 11 (Spring 1977), 3–8.

*Harris. "On *The Color Purple,* Stereotypes, and Silence." *Black American Literature Forum,* 18 (Winter 1984), 155–161.

Hellenbrand, Harold. "Speech, After Silence: AW's *The Third Life of Grange Copeland.*" *Black American Literature Forum,* 20 (Spring–Summer 1986), 113–128.

Marcus, Greil. "Limits." *New Yorker,* 52 (7 Jun 1976), 133–136. Rpt Gates & Appiah.

Mason, Theodore O, Jr. "AW's *The Third Life of Grange Copeland*: The Dynamics of Enclosure." *Callaloo,* 12 (Spring 1989), 297–309. Rpt Gates & Appiah.

McDowell, Deborah E. "The Self in Bloom: AW's *Meridian*." *College Language Association Journal,* 24 (Mar 1981), 262–275. Rpt Gates & Appiah.

*McDowell. "'The Changing Same': Generational Connections and Black Women Novelists." *New Literary History,* 18 (Winter 1987), 281–302. Rpt Bloom.

Nadel, Alan. "Reading the Body: AW's *Meridian* and the Archeology of Self." *Modern Fiction Studies,* 34 (Spring 1988), 55–68. Rpt Gates & Appiah.

*Pinckney, Darryl. "Black Victims, Black Villains." *New York Review of Books,* 34 (29 Jan 1987), 17–20.

Ross, Daniel W. "Celie in the Looking Glass: The Desire for Selfhood in *The Color Purple*." *Modern Fiction Studies,* 34 (Spring 1988), 69–84.

Royster, Philip M. "In Search of Our Fathers' Arms: AW's Persona of the Alienated Darling." *Black American Literature Forum,* 20 (Winter 1986), 347–370.

*Sadoff, Dianne F. "Black Matrilineage: The Case of AW and Zora Neale Hurston." *Signs,* 11 (Autumn 1985), 4–26. Rpt Bloom.

Stein, Karen F. "*Meridian*: AW's Critique of Revolution." *Black American Literature Forum,* 20 (Spring–Summer 1986), 129–141.

Tucker, Lindsey. "AW's *The Color Purple*: Emergent Women, Emergent Text." *Black American Literature Forum,* 22 (Spring 1988), 81–95.

Walker, Robbie. "Coping Strategies of the Women in AW's Novels: Implications for Survival." *College Language Association Journal,* 30 (Jun 1987), 401–418.

Wall, Wendy. "Lettered Bodies and Corporeal Texts in *The Color Purple*." *Studies in American Fiction,* 16 (Spring 1988), 83–97. Rpt Gates & Appiah.

Walsh, Margaret. "The Enchanted World of *The Color Purple*." *Southern Quarterly,* 25 (Winter 1987), 89–101.

Washington, J Charles. "Positive Black Male Images in AW's Fiction." *Obsidian,* 3 (Spring 1988), 23–48.

— *Craig Werner*

RICHARD WRIGHT
Near the town of Roxie, Miss, 4 Sep 1908–Paris, France, 28 Nov 1960

Richard Wright's career to 1945 brought him recognition as a writer of powerful fiction and autobiography and as a black spokesman against white racism. *Uncle Tom's Children, Native Son,* and *Black Boy,* the main works of this period, were read widely and reviewed favorably in spite of their controversial nature. During the final fifteen years of his life, spent mostly in Europe, Wright's American reputation waned, although he was highly praised by foreign critics. His concerns expanded to existentialism and Third World issues. Wright's literary artistry, racial subjects, Marxist and Freudian themes, exploration of diverse cultures, and key role in the development of African American literature continue to attract serious attention.

Bibliographies

*Davis, Charles T & Michel Fabre. *RW: A Primary Bibliography*. Boston: Hall, 1982.

*Kinnamon, Keneth, with the help of Joseph Benson, Michel Fabre & Craig Werner. *A RW Bibliography: Fifty Years of Criticism and Commentary, 1933–1982*. Westport, Conn: Greenwood, 1988.

*Kinnamon. "A Selective Bibliography of W Scholarship and Criticism, 1983–1988." *Mississippi Quarterly,* 42 (Fall 1989), 451–474.

Books

Uncle Tom's Children: Four Novellas. NY & London: Harper, 1938. Augmented as *Uncle Tom's Children: Five Long Stories*, 1940.

Native Son. NY & London: Harper, 1940. Novel.

How "Bigger" Was Born. NY & London: Harper, 1940. Essay.

Native Son (The Biography of a Young American): A Play in Ten Scenes, with Paul Green. NY & London: Harper, 1941.

12 Million Black Voices: A Folk History of the Negro in the United States. NY: Viking, 1941.

Black Boy: A Record of Childhood and Youth. NY & London: Harper, 1945. Autobiography.

The Outsider. NY: Harper, 1953. Novel.

Black Power: A Record of Reactions in a Land of Pathos. NY: Harper, 1954. Nonfiction.

Savage Holiday. NY: Avon, 1954. Novel.

The Color Curtain: A Report on the Bandung Conference. Cleveland, Ohio & NY: World, 1956.

Pagan Spain. NY: Harper, 1957. Nonfiction.

White Man, Listen! Garden City, NY: Doubleday, 1957. Essays.

The Long Dream. Garden City, NY: Doubleday, 1958. Novel.

Eight Men. Cleveland, Ohio & NY: World, 1961. Stories.

Lawd Today. NY: Walker, 1963. Novel.

American Hunger. NY & c: Harper & Row, 1977. Autobiography.

Letters

Letters to Joe C. Brown, ed with intro by Thomas Knipp. Kent, Ohio: Kent State U Libraries, 1968.

Collections

RW Reader, ed Ellen Wright & Michel Fabre. NY & c: Harper & Row, 1978.

Early Works: Lawd Today!, Uncle Tom's Children, Native Son. NY: Library of America, 1991.

Later Works: Black Boy (American Hunger), The Outsider. NY: Library of America, 1991.

Manuscripts & Archives

Beinecke Library, Yale U.

Biographies

BOOKS

*Fabre, Michel. *The Unfinished Quest of RW*. Urbana: U Illinois P, 2nd ed 1993.

Gayle, Addison. *RW: Ordeal of a Native Son*. Garden City, NY: Doubleday, 1980.

Walker, Margaret. *RW: Daemonic Genius*. NY: Warner, 1988.

Webb, Constance. *RW: A Biography*. NY: Putnam, 1968.

BOOK SECTIONS

Baldwin, James. "Princes and Powers," "The Exile," "Alas, Poor Richard." *Nobody Knows My Name* (NY: Dial, 1961), 13–55, 190–215.

Cayton, Horace R. *Long Old Road* (NY: Trident, 1965), 247–250, 253.

Davis, Allison. "Mightier Than the Sword: RW, Creator of *Native Son*." *Leadership, Love and Aggression* (NY: Harcourt Brace Jovanovich, 1983), 153–180, 248–249.

*Himes, Chester. *The Quality of Hurt: The Autobiography of Chester Himes*, Vol 1 (Garden City, NY: Doubleday, 1972), passim.

*Himes. *My Life of Absurdity* (Garden City, NY: Doubleday, 1976), passim.

ARTICLES

*Algren, Nelson. "'He Never Thanked Us for the Neckbones.'" *Chicago Tribune* (22 May 1977), Sect 7, pp 1, 8.

"Black Boy in Brooklyn." *Ebony,* 1 (Nov 1945), 26–27.

*Ellison, Ralph. "Remembering RW." *Delta,* 18 (Apr 1984), 1–13.

Harrington, Ollie "The Last Days of RW." *Ebony,* 16 (Feb 1961), 83–86, 88, 90, 92–94.

Moore, Jack B. "Black Power Revisited: In Search of RW." *Mississippi Quarterly,* 41 (Spring 1988), 161–186.

*Smith, William Gardner. "Black Boy in France." *Ebony,* 8 (Jul 1953), 32–36, 39–42.

Interviews

BOOK

*Kinnamon, Keneth & Michel Fabre, eds. *Conversations With R W*. Jackson: U P Mississippi, 1993.

Critical Studies

BOOKS

Bakish, David. *R W*. NY: Ungar, 1973.

*Bone, Robert A. *R W*. Minneapolis: U Minnesota P, 1969.

Brignano, Russell Carl. *R W: An Introduction to the Man and His Works*. Pittsburgh, Pa: U Pittsburgh P, 1970.

Butler, Robert. *Native Son: The Emergence of a New Black Hero*. Boston: Twayne, 1991.

*Fabre, Michel, *The World of R W*. Jackson: U P Mississippi, 1985.

*Fabre. *R W: Books & Writers*. Jackson: U P Mississippi, 1990.

Felgar, Robert. *R W*. Boston: Twayne, 1980.

Fishburn, Katherine. *R W's Hero: The Faces of a Rebel-Victim*. Metuchen, NJ: Scarecrow, 1977.

Joyce, Joyce Ann. *R W's Art of Tragedy*. Iowa City: U Iowa P, 1986.

*Kinnamon, Keneth. *The Emergence of R W: A Study in Literature and Society*. Urbana: U Illinois P, 1972.

Lynch, Michael F. *Creative Revolt: A Study of W, Ellison, and Dostoevsky*. NY: Lang, 1990.

Margolies, Edward. *The Art of R W*. Carbondale: Southern Illinois U P, 1969.

McCall, Dan. *The Example of R W*. NY: Harcourt, Brace & World, 1969.

Miller, Eugene E. *Voice of a Native Son: The Poetics of R W*. Jackson: U P Mississippi, 1990.

Rickels, Milton & Patricia. *R W*. Austin, Tex: Steck-Vaughn, 1970.

COLLECTIONS OF ESSAYS

Abcarian, Richard, ed. *R W's Native Son: A Critical Handbook*. Belmont, Calif: Wadsworth, 1970.

*Baker, Houston A, Jr, ed. *Twentieth Century Interpretations of Native Son*. Englewood Cliffs, NJ: Prentice-Hall, 1972.

*Bloom, Harold, ed. *RW*. NY: Chelsea House, 1987.

*Bloom, ed. *RW's Native Son*. NY: Chelsea House, 1988.

Bloom, ed. *Bigger Thomas*. NY: Chelsea House, 1990.

*Hakutani, Yoshinobu, ed. *Critical Essays on RW*. Boston: Hall, 1982.

*Kinnamon, Keneth, ed. *New Essays on Native Son*. Cambridge: Cambridge U P, 1990.

Macksey, Richard & Frank E Moorer, eds. *RW: A Collection of Critical Essays*. Englewood Cliffs, NJ: Prentice-Hall, 1984.

Ray, David & Robert M Farnsworth, eds. *RW: Impressions and Perspectives*. Ann Arbor: U Michigan P, 1973.

*Reilly, John M, ed. *RW: The Critical Reception*. NY: Franklin, 1978.

Trotman, C James, ed. *RW: Myths and Realities*. NY: Garland, 1988.

SPECIAL JOURNALS

Callaloo, 9 (Summer 1986). RW issue.

College Language Association Journal, 12 (Jun 1969). RW issue.

Mississippi Quarterly, 42 (Fall 1989). RW issue.

Negro Digest, 18 (Dec 1968). RW issue.

New Letters, 38 (Winter 1971). RW issue.

Studies in Black Literature, 1 (Autumn 1970). RW issue.

BOOK SECTIONS

Abramson, Doris E. "Broadway: *Native Son*." *Negro Playwrights in the American Theatre, 1925–1959* (NY: Columbia U P, 1969), 136–156.

*Baker, Houston A, Jr. "Racial Wisdom and RW's *Native Son*." *Long Black Song* (Charlottesville: U P Virginia, 1972), 122–141. Rpt Hakutani.

Baker. "RW and the Dynamics of Place in Afro-American Literature." Kinnamon (1990), 85–116.

*Baldwin, James. "Everybody's Protest Novel," "Many Thousands Gone." *Notes of a Native Son* (Boston: Beacon, 1955), 13–45. "Many Thousands Gone" rpt Baker, Hakutani.

*Bell, Bernard W. "RW and the Triumph of Naturalism." *The Afro-American Novel and Its Tradition* (Amherst: U Massachusetts P, 1987), 153–168.

Bigsby, C W E. "The Self and Society: RW's Dilemma." *The Second Black Renaissance* (Westport, Conn: Greenwood, 1980), 54–84.

Blake, Caesar R. "On RW's *Native Son*." *Rough Justice: Essays on Crime in Literature,* ed M L Friedland (Toronto: U Toronto P, 1991), 187–199.

Butterfield, Stephen. "RW." *Black Autobiography in America* (Amherst: U Massachusetts P, 1974), 155–179.

Cobb, Nina Kressner. "RW and the Third World." Hakutani, 228–239.

Cooke, Michael G. "Solitude: The Beginnings of Self-Realization in Zora Neale Hurston, RW, and Ralph Ellison." *Afro-American Literature in the Twentieth Century* (New Haven, Conn: Yale U P, 1984), 71–109. Rpt Bloom (1987), Bloom (1988).

*Davis, Charles T. "RW: The Artist as Public Figure," "From Experience to Eloquence: RW's *Black Boy* as Art." *Black Is the Color of the Cosmos,* ed Henry Louis Gates, Jr (NY: Garland, 1982), 271–298.

*Ellison, Ralph. "RW's Blues." *Shadow and Act* (NY: Random House, 1964), 77–94. Rpt Hakutani.

French, Warren. "The Lost Potential of RW." *The Black American Writer,* Vol 1, ed C W E Bigsby (De Land, Fla: Everett/Edwards, 1969), 125–142.

*Gayle, Addison, Jr. "The Black Rebel." *The Way of the New World* (Garden City, NY: Anchor/Doubleday, 1975), 167–202.

Gibson, Donald B. "RW: The Politics of a Lone Marxian." *The Politics of Literary Expression* (Westport, Conn: Greenwood, 1981), 21–57.

Gysin, Fritz. "RW." *The Grotesque in American Negro Fiction: Jean Toomer, RW, and Ralph Ellison* (Bern, Switz: Francke, 1975), 91–164.

Hand, Clifford. "The Struggle to Create Life in the Fiction of RW." *The Thirties,* ed Warren French (De Land, Fla: Everett/Edwards, 1967), 81–87.

Harris, Trudier. "An Anomaly in Southern Territory." *From Mammies to Militants: Domestics in Black American Literature* (Philadelphia, Pa: Temple U P, 1982), 71–86.

Harris. "Ritual Violence and the Formation of an Aesthetic." *Exorcising Blackness: Historical and Literary Lynching and Burning Rituals* (Bloomington: Indiana U P, 1984), 95–128.

Harris. "Native Sons and Foreign Daughters." Kinnamon (1990), 63–84.

JanMohamed, Abdul. "Rehistoricizing W: The Psychopolitical Function of Death in *Uncle Tom's Children*." Bloom (1987), 191–228.

JanMohamed. "Negating the Negation as a Form of Affirmation in Minority Discourse: The Construction of RW as Subject." *The Nature and*

Context of Minority Discourse, ed JanMohamed & David Lloyd (NY: Oxford U P, 1990), 102–123.

*Kent, George E. "RW: Blackness and the Adventure of Western Culture." *Blackness and the Adventure of Western Culture* (Chicago: Third World, 1972), 76–97. Rpt Baker; Macksey & Moorer; Bloom (1987).

Kinnamon, Keneth. "Call and Response: Intertextuality in Two Autobiographical Works by RW and Maya Angelou." *Studies in Black American Literature, Volume II: Belief vs. Theory in Black American Literary Criticism,* ed Joe Weixlmann & Chester J Fontenot (Greenwood, Fla: Penkevill, 1986), 121–134.

*Kinnamon. "How *Native Son* Was Born." *Writing the American Classics,* ed James Barbour & Tom Quirk (Chapel Hill: U North Carolina P, 1990), 209–234.

Klein, Marcus. "Black Boy and Native Son." *Foreigners* (Chicago: U Chicago P, 1981), 270–287.

*Lee, A Robert. "RW's Inside Narratives." *American Fiction: New Readings,* ed Richard Gray (London: Vision / Totowa, NJ: Barnes & Noble, 1983), 200–221. Rpt Bloom (1987).

*Margolies, Edward. "RW: *Native Son* and Three Kinds of Revolution." *Native Sons* (Philadelphia: Lippincott, 1968), 65–86.

Margolies. "The Letters of RW." *The Black Writer in Africa and the Americas,* ed Lloyd W Brown (Los Angeles: Hennessey & Ingalls, 1973), 101–118.

Mootry, Maria K. "Bitches, Whores, and Woman Haters: Archetypes and Typologies in the Art of RW." Macksey & Moorer, 117–127.

Porter, Horace A. "The Horror and the Glory: RW's Portrait of the Artist in *Black Boy* and *American Hunger*." Macksey & Moorer, 55–67.

Reilly, John M. "The Self-Creation of the Intellectual: *American Hunger* and *Black Power*." Hakutani, 213–227.

*Reilly. "Giving Bigger a Voice: The Politics of Narrative in *Native Son*." Kinnamon (1990), 35–62.

*Rosenblatt, Roger. "*Native Son*." *Black Fiction* (Cambridge, Mass: Harvard U P, 1974), 19–36. Rpt Bloom (1988).

Skerrett, Joseph T, Jr. "Composing Bigger: W and the Making of *Native Son*." Bloom (1988), 125–142.

Smith, Valerie. "Alienation and Creativity in the Fiction of RW." *Self-Discovery and Authority in Afro-American Narrative* (Cambridge, Mass: Harvard U P, 1987), 65–87, 161–162. Rpt Bloom (1988).

Stepto, Robert B. "Literacy and Ascent: RW's *Black Boy*." *From Behind the Veil* (Urbana: U Illinois P, 1979), 128–162. Rpt Bloom (1987).

*Van Antwerp, Margaret A, ed. "RW." *Dictionary of Literary Biography Documentary Series,* Vol 2 (Detroit, Mich: Bruccoli Clark/Gale, 1982), 397–460.

Walker, Ian. "Black Nightmare: The Fiction of RW." *Black Fiction,* ed A Robert Lee (NY: Barnes & Noble, 1980), 11–28.

Werner, Craig. "The Dangers of Domination: Joyce, Faulkner, W." *Paradoxical Resolutions* (Urbana: U Illinois P, 1982), 9–32.

*Werner. "Bigger's Blues: *Native Son* and the Articulation of Afro-American Modernism." Kinnamon (1990), 117–154.

*Williams, Sherley Anne. "Papa Dick and Sister-Woman: Reflections on Women in the Fiction of RW." *American Novelists Revisited,* ed Fritz Fleischmann (Boston: Hall, 1982), 394–415.

Young, James O. *Black Writers of the Thirties* (Baton Rouge: Louisiana State U P, 1973), passim.

ARTICLES

Adams, Timothy Dow. "I Do Believe Him Though I Know He Lies: Lying as Genre and Metaphor in RW's *Black Boy.*" *Prose Studies,* 8 (Sep 1985), 172–187.

Bone, Robert A. "RW and the Chicago Renaissance." *Callaloo,* 9 (Summer 1986), 446–468.

Brown, Lloyd W. "Stereotypes in Black and White: The Nature of Perception in W's *Native Son.*" *Black Academy Review,* 1 (Fall 1970), 35–44.

Bryant, Earle V. "Sexual Initiation and Survival in RW's *The Long Dream.*" *Southern Quarterly,* 21 (Spring 1983), 57–66.

Butler, Robert James. "The Function of Violence in RW's *Native Son.*" *Black American Literature Forum,* 20 (Spring–Summer 1986), 9–25.

Camp, Carolyn. "The Rhetoric of Catalogues in RW's *Black Boy.*" *MELUS,* 17 (Winter 1991–1992), 29–39.

Cappetti, Carla. "Sociology of an Existence: RW and the Chicago School." *MELUS,* 12 (Summer 1985), 25–43.

Coles, Robert A. "RW's Synthesis." *College Language Association Journal,* 31 (Jun 1988), 375–393.

Davis, Arthur P. "*The Outsider* as a Novel of Race." *Midwest Journal,* 7 (Winter 1956), 320–326.

DeCosta-Willis, Miriam. "Avenging Angels and Mute Mothers: Black Southern Women in W's Fictional World." *Callaloo,* 9 (Summer 1986), 540–549.

Delmar, P Jay. "Tragic Patterns in RW's *Uncle Tom's Children.*" *Negro American Literature Forum,* 10 (Spring 1976), 3–12.

Emanuel, James. "Fever and Feeling: Notes on the Imagery in *Native Son.*" *Negro Digest,* 18 (Dec 1968), 16–24. Rpt Abcarian.

France, Alan W. "Misogyny and Appropriation in W's *Native Son.*" *Modern Fiction Studies,* 34 (Autumn 1988), 413–423.

Gelfant, Blanche. "Residence Underground: Recent Fictions of the Subterranean City." *Sewanee Review,* 83 (Jul–Sep 1975), 406–438.

*Gibson, Donald B. "W's Invisible Native Son." *American Quarterly,* 21 (Winter 1969), 728–738. Rpt Baker; Macksey & Moorer.

Gibson. "RW and the Tyranny of Convention." *College Language Association Journal,* 12 (Jun 1969), 344–357.

Gibson. "RW's *Black Boy* and the Trauma of Autobiographical Rebirth." *Callaloo,* 9 (Summer 1986), 492–498.

Graves, Neil. "RW's Unheard Melodies: The Songs of *Uncle Tom's Children.*" *Phylon,* 40 (Sep 1979), 278–290.

Hakutani, Yoshinobu. "RW and American Naturalism." *Zeitschrift für Anglistik und Amerikanistik,* 36 (Third Quarter 1988), 217–226.

Hoeveler, Diane Long. "Oedipus Agonistes: Mothers and Sons in RW's Fiction." *Black American Literature Forum,* 12 (Summer 1978), 65–68.

Holladay, Hilary. "*Native Son*'s Guilty Man." *CEA Critic,* 54 (Winter 1992), 30–36.

Howard, William. "RW's Flood Stories and the Great Mississippi River Flood of 1927: Social and Historical Backgrounds." *Southern Literary Journal,* 16 (Spring 1984), 44–62.

*Howe, Irving. "Black Boys and Native Sons." *Dissent,* 10 (Autumn 1963), 353–368. Rpt Abcarian, Baker, Hakutani.

Hurd, Myles Raymond. "Between Blackness and Bitonality: W's 'Long Black Song.'" *College Language Association Journal,* 35 (Sep 1991), 42–56.

Jackson, Blyden. "RW in a Moment of Truth." *Southern Literary Journal,* 3 (Spring 1971), 3–17. Rpt Macksey & Moorer.

*Kazin, Alfred. "Too Honest for His Own Time." *New York Times Book Review* (29 Dec 1991), 3, 17–18.*Kinnamon, Keneth. "*Native Son:* The Personal, Social, and Political Background." *Phylon,* 30 (Spring 1969), 66–72. Rpt Abcarian; Hakutani; Macksey & Moorer.

Kinnamon. "Isolation and Community in RW's *American Hunger.*" *Minority Voices,* 1 (Fall 1977), 104–106.

Kostelanetz, Richard. "The Politics of Unresolved Quests in the Novels of RW." *Xavier Review,* 8 (Spring 1969), 31–64.

Liebowitz, Herbert. "RW's *Black Boy:* Styles of Deprivation." *Southwest Review,* 70 (Winter 1985), 71–94.

Liebowitz. "Arise Ye Pris'ners of Starvation: On RW's *American Hunger.*" *Pequod,* 23–24 (1987), 250–265.

Lowe, John. "W Writing Reading: Narrative Strategies in *Uncle Tom's Children.*" *Journal of the Short Story in English,* 11 (Autumn 1988), 49–74.

Margolies, Edward. "RW's Opposing Freedoms." *Mississippi Quarterly,* 42 (Fall 1989), 409–414.

Mayberry, Susan Neal. "Symbols in the Sewer: A Symbolic Renunciation of Symbols in RW's 'The Man Who Lived Underground.'" *South Atlantic Review,* 54 (Jan 1989), 71–83.

McCarthy, B Eugene. "Models of History in RW's *Uncle Tom's Children.*" *Black American Literature Forum,* 25 (Winter 1991), 729–743.

Mechling, Jay. "The Failure of Folklore in RW's *Black Boy.*" *Journal of American Folklore,* 104 (Summer 1991), 275–294.

Miller, James A. "Bigger Thomas's Quest for Voice and Audience in RW's *Native Son.*" *Callaloo,* 9 (Summer 1986), 501–506.

Moore, Jack B. "RW's Dream of Africa." *Journal of African Studies,* 2 (Summer 1975), 231–245.

Moore. "The Art of *Black Power*: Novelistic or Documentary." *Revue Française d'Etudes Américaines,* 12 (Feb 1987), 79–91.

Nagel, James. "Images of 'Vision' in *Native Son.*" *University Review,* 36 (Dec 1969), 109–115. Rpt Hakutani.

Ochschorn, Kathleen. "The Community of *Native Son.*" *Mississippi Quarterly,* 42 (Fall 1989), 387–392.

Pudaloff, Ross. "Celebrity as Identity: RW, *Native Son,* and Mass Culture." *Studies in American Fiction,* 11 (Spring 1983), 3–18.

*Rampersad, Arnold. "Too Honest for His Own Time." *New York Times Book Review* (29 Dec 1991), 3, 18–19.

*Reilly, John M. "Self-Portraits by RW." *Colorado Quarterly,* 20 (Summer 1971), 31–45.

Reilly. "RW's Apprenticeship." *Journal of Black Studies,* 2 (Jun 1972), 439–460.

Reilly. "RW's Curious Thriller *Savage Holiday.*" *College Language Association Journal,* 21 (Dec 1977), 218–223.

Reilly. "RW's Discovery of the Third World." *Minority Voices,* 2 (Fall 1978), 47–53.

Reilly. "RW and the Art of Non-Fiction: Stepping Out on the Stage of the World." *Callaloo,* 9 (Summer 1986), 507–520.

Scott, Nathan A. "Search for Beliefs: Fiction of RW." *University of Kansas City Review,* 23 (Autumn–Winter 1956), 19–24, 131–138.

*Scott. "The Dark and Haunted Tower of RW." *Graduate Comment,* 7 (Jul 1964), 93–99. Rpt Macksey & Moorer.

Sillen, Samuel. "The Meaning of Bigger Thomas." *New Masses,* 35 (Apr 1940), 26–28.

*Skerrett, Joseph T, Jr. "RW, Writing and Identity." *Callaloo,* 2 (Oct 1979), 84–94.

Smith, Sidonie Ann. "RW's *Black Boy:* The Creative Impulse as Rebellion." *Southern Literary Journal,* 5 (Fall 1972), 123–136.

*Stepto, Robert B. "I Thought I Knew These People: RW & the Afro-American Literary Tradition." *Massachusetts Review,* 18 (Autumn 1977), 525–541. Rpt Bloom (1987).

Tate, Claudia C. "Christian Existentialism in RW's *The Outsider.*" *College Language Association Journal,* 25 (Jun 1982), 371–395.

*Thaddeus, Janice. "The Metamorphosis of RW's *Black Boy.*" *American Literature,* 57 (May 1985), 199–214.

Turner, Darwin T. "*The Outsider:* Revision of an Idea." *College Language Association Journal,* 12 (Jun 1969), 310–321. Rpt Macksey & Moorer.

Tuttleton, James W. "The Problematic Texts of RW." *Hudson Review,* 45 (Summer 1992), 261–271.

Watkins, Patricia D. "The Paradoxical Structure of RW's 'The Man Who Lived Underground.'" *Black American Literature Forum,* 23 (Winter 1989), 767–783.

Webb, Tracy. "The Role of Water Imagery in *Uncle Tom's Children.*" *Modern Fiction Studies,* 34 (Spring 1988), 5–16.

Wertham, Frederic. "An Unconscious Determinant in *Native Son.*" *Journal of Clinical Psychopathology and Psychotherapy,* 6 (Jul 1944), 111–115.

Williams, John A. "RW: The Legacy of a Native Son." *Washington Post Book World* (22 Sep 1992), 1, 10.

Winslow, Henry F. "R Nathaniel W: Destroyer and Preserver (1908–1960)." *Crisis,* 69 (Mar 1962), 149–163, 187.

— *Keneth Kinnamon*

A CHECKLIST FOR STUDENTS OF AMERICAN FICTION

Sixty-eight works and five periodicals essential to the study of modern American fiction.

These reference sources are intended to aid research on general aspects of American literature and its connections with other fields. Tools specific to genres, periods, and authors are listed under those rubrics in the appropriate *Essential Bibliography of American Fiction* volumes.

Historical Background

1. *American Studies: An Annotated Bibliography,* ed Jack Salzman. Cambridge: Cambridge U P, 1986. 3 vols. Supplement, 1990.
   Summaries of books on U.S. society & culture; well-organized, useful index.
2. *Dictionary of American Biography,* ed Allen Johnson, Dumas Malone et al. NY: Scribners, 1928– . 20 vols, 8 supplements & index.
   Generally excellent scholarly essays with brief bibliographies.
3. *Dictionary of American History,* ed Louise B Katz. NY: Scribners, 1976–1978. 7 vols & index.
   Careful identification of events, places & movements. For biographies, use *DAB* (#2).
4. *Encyclopedia of American Facts and Dates* by Gorton Carruth. 8th ed, NY: Harper & Row, 1987.
   Best chronology of American history.
5. *Guide to the Study of the United States of America: Representative Books Reflecting the Development of American Life and Thought,* ed Roy P Basler et al. Washington: Library of Congress, 1960. Supplement, 1976.
   Annotated list of titles.
6. *Harvard Guide to American History,* ed Frank Freidel. Cambridge: Harvard U P, rev 1974. 2 vols.
   Selective topical bibliographies.

7. *Oxford Companion to American History,* ed Thomas H Johnson. NY: Oxford U P, 1966.
8. *Oxford History of the American People* by Samuel Eliot Morison. NY: Oxford U P, 1965.

The American Language

9. *The American Language: An Inquiry into the Development of English in the United States* by H L Mencken. 4th ed, NY: Knopf, 1936. Supplements, 1945 & 1948.
   Personalized narrative on history & quirks of written & spoken American English.
10. *Dictionary of American English on Historical Principles,* ed William A Craigie & James R Hulbert. Chicago: U Chicago P, 1938–1944. 4 vols. American complement to *OED* (#12).
11. *New Dictionary of American Slang,* ed Robert L Chapman. NY: Harper & Row, 1986.
12. *Oxford English Dictionary.* 2nd ed, ed J A Simpson & E S C Weiner, Oxford: Oxford U P, 1989. 20 vols. †
   A historical dictionary, chronicling meanings & usage of 500,000 words over a millenium. Heavily British, so balanced by Craigie & Hulbert (#10).

Literature

QUOTATIONS

13. *Familiar Quotations: A Collection of Passages, Phrases and Proverbs Traced to their Sources in Ancient and Modern Literature* by John Bartlett. 16th ed, ed Justin Kaplan et al. Boston: Little, Brown, 1992.
   Standard, updated compilation, arranged by author & date; well-indexed.
14. *A New Dictionary of Quotations on Historical Principles From Ancient and Modern Sources* by H L Mencken. NY: Knopf, 1942.
   Among the many books of quotations, this may rank highest for literary interest.

---

† Daggers indicate works that are at least partly available by computer. See note on "Computer Availability" at the end of this checklist.

LITERARY HISTORIES

15. *Annals of American Literature 1602–1983,* ed Richard M Ludwig & Clifford A Nault, Jr. NY: Oxford U P, 1986.
    Chronology of significant literary events & publications.
16. *Cambridge History of American Literature,* ed William Peterfield Trent el al. Cambridge: Cambridge U P / NY: Putnam, 1917–1921. 4 vols.
    Exhaustive treatment for 17th through 19th centuries.
17. *Literary History of the United States: History.* 4th ed, ed Robert E Spiller et al. NY: Macmillan / London: Collier Macmillan, 1974.
    Particularly strong for pre–World War I literature & background. See # 45.

LITERARY DICTIONARIES

18. *Benét's Reader's Encyclopedia of American Literature,* ed George Perkins, Barbara Perkins & Philip Leininger. NY: Harper Collins, 1991.
    Lively discussion of authors, terms & historical allusions.
19. *A Handbook to Literature* by C Hugh Holman. 6th ed, NY: Macmillan, 1992.
    Essential dictionary of literary terminology. Comprehensive, with useful appendixes.
20. *Oxford Companion to American Literature.* 5th ed, ed James D Hart, NY: Oxford U P, 1983.
    Oxford Companions are standards of pithy identifications of authors, works, characters in literature & may also contain useful appendixes.

LITERARY BIOGRAPHIES

21. *American Women Writers: A Critical Reference Guide From Colonial Times to the Present,* ed Lina Mainiero. NY: Ungar, 1979-1982. 4 vols.
    Critical biography & selected bibliography for 1,000 writers, many not covered elsewhere.
22. *American Writers.* NY: Scribners, 1974. 4 vols. 2-vol supplements, 1979, 1981, 1991.
    Scholarly essays with selective bibliographies. Based on the *U Minnesota Pamphlets on American Writers.*
23. *Black American Writers, Past and Present: A Biographical and Bibliographical Dictionary,* ed Theressa Gunnels Rush et al. Metuchen, NJ: Scarecrow, 1975.
    Uneven guide to 2,000 writers.

24. *Contemporary Authors: A Bio-Bibliographical Guide to Current Writers in Fiction, General NonFiction, Poetry, Journalism, Drama, Motion Pictures, Television, and Other Fields.* Detroit, Mich: Gale, 1962– . 160 vols to date. [†]

Biographical, occasionally critical information, regularly revised, very current. *Bibliographic Series,* 2 volumes to date, provides extensive bibliographies on authors.

25. *Dictionary of Literary Biography.* Detroit, Mich: Bruccoli Clark Layman/Gale, 1978– . 162 vols to date.

Scholarly, illustrated, critical-biographical essays with bibliographies. Individual volumes cover international literatures by nationality, genre & period. Includes *Yearbooks* and *Documentary Series* volumes. Also *Concise Dictionary of American Literary Biography,* 1987–1989, 6 vols. Cumulatively indexed.

26. *Twentieth Century Authors,* ed Stanley J Kunitz & Howard Haycraft. NY: Wilson, 1942. Supplement, ed Kunitz & Vineta Colby, 1955.

27. *World Authors, 1950–1970,* ed John Wakeman. NY: Wilson, 1975. Supplements, *1970–1975* (1980); *1975–1980,* ed Vineta Colby (1985); *1980–1985,* ed Colby (1991).

PRIMARY BIBLIOGRAPHIES

28. *Bibliography of American Literature,* ed Jacob Blanck. New Haven, Conn: Yale U P, 1955–1991. 9 vols.

Primary bibliographies of books by nearly 300 authors who died before 1931.

29. *Books in Print.* NY: Bowker, 1948– . Annually with updates. [†]

Listing by author, title & subject of books available from or projected by major American publishers.

30. *Cumulative Book Index.* NY: Wilson, 1933– . Quarterly, cumulated annually.[†]

English-language books published internationally. See # 37.

31. *First Printings of American Authors: Contributions Toward Descriptive Checklists.* Detroit, Mich: Bruccoli Clark/Gale, 1977–1987. 5 vols.

Listings for many authors not found elsewhere.

32. *Facts On File Bibliography of American Fiction: 1919–1988,* 2 vols, ed Matthew J Bruccoli & Judith S Baughman; *1866–1918,* 1 vol, ed James Nagel & Gwen L Nagel; *1588–1865,* 1 vol, ed Kent P Lungquist. NY: Manly/Facts On File, 1991–1993.

Listings of books by & selected criticism of authors between 1588 and 1988.

33. *National Union Catalog, Pre-1956 Imprints.* London: Mansell, 1968–1980. 685 vols. Supplementary vols 686–754.

Listing by author of all books published before 1956 & owned by American research libraries, including the Library of Congress. Basic bibliographical information with locations.

34. *National Union Catalog, 1956–1967,* 125 vols, Totowa, NJ: Rowman & Littlefield, 1972; *1968–1972,* 104 vols, Ann Arbor, Mich: Edwards, 1973; *1973–1977,* 135 vols, Totowa, NJ: Rowman & Littlefield, 1978. Annual, 1974– .
   Continuation of # 33 in book form; since 1983 issued on microfiche. Large portion of NUC available in MARC database.

35. *New Serial Titles, 1950–70: A Union List of Serials Commencing Publication after December 31, 1949.* Washington: Library of Congress, 1973. 4 vols. Updates: *1971–75* (1976), 2 vols; *1976–80* (1981), 2 vols; *1981–85* (1986), 6 vols; *1986–89* (1990), 6 vols.

36. *Union List of Serials in Libraries of the United States and Canada.* 3rd ed, NY: Wilson, 1965. 5 vols.
   Limited by age, but best listing of major libraries' holdings of journals that began before 1950.

37. *United States Catalog: Books in Print.* NY: Wilson, 1899–1928. 4 vols, 7 supplements.
   Periodic cumulation from publishers' catalogues, arranged by author, title & subject. Continued by *CBI* (# 30).

38. *United States Newspaper Program National Union List.* 3rd ed, Dublin, Ohio: OCLC, 1989.
   Ongoing cooperative listing of all library holdings, with locations & exact holdings, both paper & microfilm.

INDEXES TO PRIMARY SOURCES

39. *Reader's Guide to Periodical Literature: An Author and Subject Index.* NY: Wilson, 1900– . Monthly, with quarterly & annual cumulations. †
   Guide to popular, nontechnical magazines.

40. *Short Story Index: An Index to Stories in Collections and Periodicals.* NY: Wilson, 1953– .
   Annual, periodic cumulations.

BIBLIOGRAPHIES OF CRITICISM

41. *The American Novel 1789–1959: A Checklist of Twentieth-Century Criticism* by Donna L Gerstenberger & George Hendrick. Denver: Swallow, 1961. *Volume II: Criticism Written 1960–1968,* Chicago: Swallow, 1970.
   Listing by novelist & by novel. Good starting point.

42. *American Short-Fiction Criticism and Scholarship, 1959–1977: A Checklist* by Joe Weixlmann. Chicago: Swallow, 1982.
   Comprehensive, accurate & usable.

43. *Articles on Twentieth-Century Literature: An Annotated Bibliography, 1954–70,* ed David E Pownall. Millwood, NY: Kraus, 1973–1980. 7 vols.
    International in scope of subjects & journals indexed.
44. *The Contemporary Novel: A Checklist of Critical Literature on the British and American Novel Since 1945* by Irving Adelman & Rita Dworkin. Metuchen, NJ: Scarecrow, 1972.
    Criticism of 200 authors, listed by novelist & novel.
45. *Literary History of the United States: Bibliography.* 4th ed, ed Robert E Spiller et al. NY: Macmillan / London: Collier Macmillan, 1974.
    Awkward but important combination of three previously published bibliographies covering pre-1948, 1948–1958, 1958–1970. See # 17.
46. *Short Fiction Criticism: A Checklist of Interpretation Since 1925 of Stories and Novelettes (American, British, Continental), 1800–1958,* ed Jarvis Thurston et al. Denver: Swallow, 1960.
    Useful for early criticism; updated by Weixlmann (# 42).
47. *Sixteen Modern American Authors: A Survey of Research and Criticism,* ed Jackson R Bryer. Durham, NC: Duke U P, rev 1974. Vol 2 (1989) covers 1972–1988.
    S Anderson, Cather, S Crane, Dreiser, Eliot, Faulkner, Fitzgerald, Frost, Hemingway, O'Neill, Pound, Robinson, Steinbeck, Stevens, W C Williams & Wolfe.
48. *Twentieth-Century Short Story Explication, 1900–1975* by Warren S Walker. 3rd ed, Hamden, Conn: Shoe String, 1977. Supplements, *1976–1978* (1980), *1977–1981* (1984), *1981–1984* (1987), *1984–1986* (1989), *1987–1988* (1991). Index (1992).
    Extensive, but difficult to use. Journal abbreviations defined in supplements.

PERIODICAL GUIDES TO CRITICISM

49. *Abstracts of English Studies.* Calgary: U Calgary P, 1958– . Quarterly
    International guide to articles & essays, many not indexed elsewhere, on English & American literature.
50. *American Literary Scholarship.* Durham, NC: Duke U P, 1965– . Annual.
    Bibliographic essays on genres, authors, periods.
51. *Annual Bibliography of English Language and Literature.* Cambridge, UK: Modern Humanities Research Association, 1920– . Annual.
    International, arranged by topic. Supplements *MLAIB* (#57).
52. *Book Review Digest.* NY: Wilson, 1905– . 10 times per year, cumulated annually. †
    Excerpts from reviews of popular books in magazines & newspapers.
53. *Book Review Index.* Detroit, Mich: Gale, 1965– . Bi-monthly, cumulated.†
    Far more comprehensive than #52; especially good for scholarly books & novels receiving limited attention.

54. *Combined Retrospective Index to Book Reviews in Humanities Journals, 1802–1974*. Woodbridge, Conn: Research Publications, 1982–1984. 10 vols.

    500,000 reviews from 150 journals listed; especially strong in literature.

55. *Contemporary Literary Criticism: Excerpts From the Criticism of Today's Novelists, Poets, Playwrights and Other Creative Writers*. Detroit, Mich: Gale, 1973– .

    International coverage, long excerpts from criticism. Format similar to *TCLC* (#58).

56. *Humanities Index*. NY: Wilson, 1974– . Quarterly, cumulated annually. †

    Not as comprehensive as *MLAIB* (#57), but interdisciplinary, covering history, philosophy, theology, as well as language & literature. Valuable for timeliness. Supersedes *International Index* (1907–1965) & *Social Sciences and Humanities Index* (1965–1974).

57. *MLA International Bibliography of Books and Articles on the Modern Languages and Literature*. NY: MLA, 1921– . Annual. †

    Extensive, international coverage of American literature & since 1981 enhanced by subject index. Arrangement by nationality & period. Must be supplemented by other indexes.

58. *Twentieth-Century Literary Criticism: Excerpts From Criticism of the Works of Novelists, Poets, Playwrights, Short Story Writers, and Other Creative Writers, 1900–1960, From the First Published Critical Appraisals to Current Evaluations*. Detroit, Mich: Gale, 1978– .

GUIDES TO RESEARCH

59. *Bibliographical Guide to the Study of the Literature of the U.S.A.* by Clarence L Gohdes & Sanford E Marovitz. 5th ed, Durham, NC: Duke U P, 1984.

    Annotated listing, especially good for topical approach.

60. *Literary Research Guide: A Guide to Reference Sources for the Study of Literatures in English and Related Topics* by James L Harner. NY: MLA, 1989.

    Useful manual for using the library. Hundreds of annotations on selected reference books; appendixes.

BOOKS & PUBLISHING

61. *The Book in America: A History of the Making and Selling of Books in the United States* by Hellmut Lehmann-Haupt et al. 2nd ed, NY: Bowker, 1952.

62. *Glaister's Glossary of the Book* by Geoffrey Ashall Glaister. 2nd ed, London: Allen & Unwin, 1979.
    Treats all aspects of the book & publishing. Illustrations & appendixes.
63. *Guide to the Study of United States Imprints* by G Thomas Tanselle. Cambridge: Harvard U P, 1971. 2 vols.
    Comprehensive checklists of materials on all aspects of printing & publishing history. See also *DLB* (#25), vol 46.
64. *A History of American Magazines* by Frank Luther Mott. Cambridge: Harvard U P, 1938–1968. 5 vols.
    Covers 1741–1930, by period, genre & specific titles.
65. *History of Book Publishing in the United States* by John W Tebbel. NY: Bowker, 1973–1981. 4 vols.

DIRECTORIES

66. *Literary Market Place: The Directory of American Book Publishing.* NY: Bowker, 1940- . Annual.
    Addresses & information for publishers, agents, reviewers, book clubs, etc.
67. *MLA Directory of Periodicals: A Guide to Journals and Series in Languages and Literatures.* NY: MLA, 1979–. Annual.
    Listing of all serials indexed by *MLAIB* (#57).
68. *Ulrich's International Periodicals Directory.* NY: Bowker, 1932- . Annual. †
    Best listing of currently published titles by subject; valuable for listing of indexes that cover each journal.

Important Journals

J-1. *American Literature: A Journal of Literary History, Criticism, and Bibliography.* Durham, NC: Duke U P, 1929- . Quarterly.
    Critical articles, book reviews, research in progress; formerly thorough, now selective bibliography.
J-2. *American Quarterly.* Philadelphia: U Pennsylvania P, 1949- . Quarterly.
    Explores the cultural background of literature. Bibliographical essays.
J-3. *Modern Fiction Studies.* West Lafayette, Ind: Purdue U, Department of English, 1955- . Quarterly.
J-4. *Resources for American Literary Study.* College Park: U Maryland, Department of English, 1971- . Semiannual.

J-5. *Studies in American Fiction*. Boston: Northeastern U, Department of English, 1973– . Semiannual.

— Daniel Boice

COMPUTER AVAILABILITY

Reference works for American fiction are increasingly available through computer technology. Some are accessible on CD-ROM or on computerized catalogues of large libraries. Others are "on-line" tools, which are used via telephone linkage to computer centers or databases. More and more tools can be used in several of these formats, and reference librarians can advise on which tools are available at individual libraries.

Advantages of computerized resources include speed, ability to look for several topics at once, and printing out of citations. Factors that determine the usefulness of these tools include the reliability of both data and method, ease of use, and especially scope—that is, how broadly the tool covers the subject and what years and journals it indexes. Many computerized tools cover only recent years and must be supplemented by using printed versions.

Titles in the Checklist that are at least partially available by computer are marked by daggers (†). Reference librarians will be able to provide advice and direction. Other major computer tools include:

OCLC (Online Computer Library Center): A network including nearly all American libraries and many foreign ones. Lists millions of books, journals, maps, recordings and archival materials. Especially useful for identifying libraries with specific titles.

RLIN (Research Libraries Network): Listing of items held by the leading American research libraries, the Research Libraries Group. Good for all library materials, especially archives.

Both the *OCLC* and *RLIN* databases include the recent Library of Congress cataloguing, called *MARC* (Machine Readable Cataloguing). The strength of *OCLC* is its broad coverage of libraries, but *RLIN* is more careful in its cataloguing. Both *RLIN* and *OCLC* offer several ways to locate books, beyond the traditional avenues of author and title. Librarians will provide information regarding availability of these tools.

— *Daniel Boice*

MODERN AFRICAN AMERICAN WRITERS:
Basic Literary Histories, Bibliographies & Biographical Sources

Baker, Houston A, Jr. *Singers of Daybreak: Studies in Black American Literature*. Washington: Howard U P, 1974.

Bell, Bernard W. *The Afro-America Novel and Its Tradition*. Amherst: U Massachusetts P, 1987.

Bone, Robert. *The Negro Novel in America*. New Haven, Conn: Yale U P, rev 1965.

Davis, Arthur P. *From the Dark Tower: Afro-American Writers, 1900 to 1960*. Washington: Howard U P, 1974.

Davis, Thadious M & Trudier Harris, eds. *Dictionary of Literary Biography, Volume Thirty-three: Afro-American Fiction Writers After 1955*. Detroit, Mich: Bruccoli Clark/Gale, 1984.

Draper, James P, ed. *Black Literature Criticism*. Detroit, Mich: Gale, 1992. 3 vols.

Gayle, Addison, Jr. *The Way of the New World: The Black Novel in American*. Garden City, NY: Anchor/Doubleday, 1975.

Harris, Norman. *Connecting Times: The Sixties in Afro-American Fiction*. Jackson: U P Mississippi, 1988.

Harris, Trudier, ed. *Dictionary of Literary Biography, Volume Fifty-one: Afro-American Writers From the Harlem Renaissance to 1940*. Detroit, Mich: Bruccoli Clark/Gale, 1987.

Harris. *Dictionary of Literary Biography, Volume Seventy-Six: Afro-American Writers, 1940–1995*. Detroit, Mich: Bruccoli Clark Layman/Gale, 1988.

Houston, Helen Ruth. *The Afro-American Novel 1965–1975: A Descriptive Bibliography of Primary and Secondary Materials*. Troy, NY: Whitston, 1977.

Lee, A Robert. *Black Fiction: New Studies in the Afro-American Novel Since 1945*. NY: Barnes & Noble, 1980.

Margolies, Edward. *Native Sons: A Critical Study of Twentieth-Century Negro American Authors*. Philadelphia: Lippincott, 1968.

Rosenblatt, Roger. *Black Fiction*. Cambridge, Mass: Harvard U P, 1974.

Shockley, Ann Allen & Sue P Chandler. *Living Black American Authors: A Biographical Directory*. NY: Bowker, 1973.

Smith, Valerie & Lea Baechler & A Walton Litz, eds. *African American Writers*. NY: Scribners, 1991.

Werner, Craig. *Black American Women Authors: An Annotated Bibliography*. Pasadena, Calif & Englewood Cliffs, NJ: Salem, 1989.

— Daniel Boice

INDEX

Writers' names appear in **boldface**.

Y